San Francisco Bay Area

LandMarks

REFLECTIONS OF FOUR CENTURIES

Text and photography by
Charles Kennard

Foreword by James D. Houston

Tioga Publishing Company
Palo Alto, California

ACKNOWLEDGMENTS

My greatest indebtedness is to those historians whose works have led me to the more eloquent of the myriad of source documents. To the creators and personnel of the federal, state, and regional parks and open-space districts, much appreciation is due for the preservation of a rich legacy; many of the photographs were taken on these lands, frequently with the kind cooperation of park employees.

The staff members of many museums and libraries have been ever diligent and patient in giving assistance: special thanks to Jocelyn Moss and her staff at the main branch of the Marin County Public Library and to the staff of the San Francisco Archives, who never failed to brighten sometimes tedious work; also to Robin Wells of the Treganza Museum of Anthropology at San Francisco State University, Sarah Conklin of the National Maritime Museum, Dave Herod of the Lowie Museum of Anthropology at the University of California, Berkeley, and Lorelei Corcoran Schwabe of Old Mission San Jose.

I thank also the publishers and others who gave permission to reprint excerpts from their books or documents; individual acknowledgments appear in Sources and Locations at the back of this book.

Behind many a photograph is a story of people who generously went out of their way to help me with their time, expertise, contacts, and resources. A thank you also to those who do not have the gratification of seeing the photography in which they assisted represented in the final selection.

Much credit is due to my publisher, Karen Nilsson, who with faith and tact guided the project into coherent form, and to Mary Anne Stewart, my editor, who tirelessly pressed for intelligibility and consistency in all aspects of the book. Design was in the careful and talented hands of Jon Goodchild of Triad.

My appreciation goes to those who reviewed and commented on the manuscript at various stages: John Hart, Eleanor Huggins, Judith Kunofsky, Malcolm Margolin, Larry Orman, and especially Richard Dillon.

During the four years this book has been in the making, many people have given much-needed encouragement; I am very grateful to them all, particularly David Goldberg.

Above all, my gratitude goes to my muse, editor, and wife, Eva Seligman Kennard.

LIBRARY OF CONGRESS CATALOGING-IN-PUBLICATION DATA
Kennard, Charles, 1952–
San Francisco Bay Area Landmarks.
Bibliography: p. 157.
Includes index.
1. Historic sites—California—San Francisco Bay Area—Pictorial works. 2. San Francisco Bay Area (Calif.)—Description and travel—Views.
I. Title.
F868.S156K44   1987   979.4′6   87-14647

ISBN 0-935382-63-1

Tioga Publishing Company
P.O. Box 98
Palo Alto, California 94302

Distributed by William Kaufmann, Inc.
P.O. Box 50490
Palo Alto, California 94303

First printing

Designed and produced by
Jon Goodchild/Triad
Typeset by TBD Typography, San Rafael

Printed in Japan

to my father
Robert William Kennard

Contents

Foreword

The first time I looked through the pages of this book and felt its spirit, I was reminded of a scene at the county courthouse here in Santa Cruz back in 1970. It was a public hearing to debate the future of a piece of shoreline located about sixty-five miles south of San Francisco. The issue: should the county allow an eastern development corporation to erect five thousand houses on a 650-acre tract of ocean frontage? Most of this acreage was coastal terrace ideal for broccoli and brussels sprouts and generally considered to be among the numerous and irreplacable treasures that make the coast of California unique in the world.

A hundred people were packed into the room and spilling out the doors—attorneys, high school students, housewives, professors, real estate agents, retired folks from the trailer courts—most of them there to oppose the plan. The arguments were the familiar ones: projections of inevitable growth versus environmental overload and quality of life; the revenue from an expanded tax base versus impact on existing roads and sewers and water supply.

Midway through the hearing an elderly man appeared at the microphone. He wore a trenchcoat, looked a bit like Igor Stravinsky, with gray tousled hair and eyes that took command of the crowd.

"My name is Ransom Rideout," he began. "I am the oldest man in this room. I was born in San Francisco in 1889. I can remember as a boy traveling out Mission Street as far as the city extended, out to about Twenty-first Street in those days. Then the Italian vegetable gardens began. And there were windmills out there, hundreds and hundreds of windmills spinning above those gardens."

His voice was as compelling as his eyes. Somehow it conveyed both nostalgia and urgency.

"When I was fourteen I saw my first lion. And you want to know where it was? It was in Wildcat Canyon. Right over the hill from where the Berkeley campus is now. Mountain lions were roaming those hills—*in my time!*

"When I was a little older my father bought a beautiful piece of farmland down in the richest valley in the world. The Santa Clara Valley. And we raised crops there until the state came along and decided to run the Nimitz Freeway through the middle of our acreage. Just cut it in two. I can drive up to Oakland along that freeway now and look out and see storage tanks where our artesian well used to be. The underground pressure in that well was so strong we didn't need any pumps. The water just flowed free. That's all paved over now. . . ."

He continued, citing other losses he had lived through, and while he talked, the room was dead silent. Speeches had been limited to five minutes. Rideout talked for ten before the chairman asked him how much more he had to say. When he said just a couple of points, the chairman sat back and waited, causing me to wonder what kind of clout this old man had with the board.

"In my time, gentlemen," he said, "I have seen Eden. EDEN! Just three weeks ago I was camping overnight up the coast here a ways, not far from Año Nuevo Island, and I probably shouldn't tell you what I saw when I woke up that morning, because someone might decide to go out and shoot that beautiful creature. . . ."

His voice fell to a gravelly smoothness as he caressed the words. "I saw a mountain lion. Not thirty yards from where I was sleeping. And that animal just loped away from me, into the brush."

There was a long pause, a reverent silence, while we all waited. I'm sure he had used the word *Eden* by design. He knew what would move us. Which is not to say that the shoreline and the rippled Coast Ranges north and south of San Francisco are paradise. Far from it. But they represent something potent in our collective imagination, something that is both generous and wild, and a source of *re-creation* in the most literal sense.

"That was just three weeks ago," he said, "and not very far at all from this room. It was right over there."

He pointed north and west, up the coast, in the direction of the crop-laden terraces where — according to someone else's version of the land of promise — five thousand interchangeable houses were programmed to appear in long curving rows.

When he sat down everyone in the room stood up, including the board members. The applause lasted about two minutes. And it was clear then what the old man had done. He had been speaking for everyone. At such meetings there is always a tendency on the part of the dissenting public to see any commission or hearing board as the adversary. Somehow, during his twelve minutes or so at the microphone, Rideout erased that. The subject, for him, was more than the fate of 950 acres. It was the fate of landscape and open spaces in all the growth-pressured counties that fan out from San Francisco Bay. The paving over of his family's artesian well was but one of the prophetic moments in his long life. He had lived through, many times, what every person who has been in California for half a year has lived through at least once. The board members let him have his long say because he seemed to be the voice of history itself, and because they too were ready to hear his cry, let him bear witness for all of us in that room.

Rideout was a Californian by birth, and his sense of loss ran deep because the love for his home region ran so deep. Charles Kennard is another kind of Californian, the kind who has arrived here from somewhere else, to discover the Bay Area as if for the first time, to choose it, and then to fall in love with the place, or rather, with the rich abundance of places that are acknowledged and depicted in this book.

What makes his love affair unusual, in my view, is his remarkable sense of history. For a variety of reasons, this sense is rare out west. The region has a marvelous history, but not many of those who live here are in touch with it. The Bay Area continues to be a land of immigrants, filled with people who have come here, from every direction, in order to leave some past behind and make a new start. Meanwhile, even if you have spent your life here, accelerated change is as much a part of the atmosphere as the celebrated California Dream itself. In the course of twenty-five years or so you can watch a piece of orchard become a service station, which becomes a Jack-in-the-Box, which becomes a savings and loan. In such a realm one can easily forget how things looked six months or a year ago, let alone what might have happened in 1959 or 1859.

In this book Charles Kennard gives us two things at once — a persuasive grasp of the Bay Area's complex past, and the fresh perspective of someone who has discovered California within the past ten years. For me, it has been an illumination. The region he has documented is the part of the world I consider home. I was born in San Francisco, finished high school and college in Santa Clara Valley. Most of my life has been spent between Marin County and Monterey Bay. And yet, through his eyes, I am seeing this world again, seeing it anew.

The way certain angles of vision are reversed, for example, is particularly refreshing. A profile of Mount Tamalpais across a meadow is followed, a few pages later, by a distant view of the bay as seen beyond a stone outcropping at the top of the legendary mountain. A panorama of the Fort Ross stockade is followed by a moody interior shot out a window toward a building across the compound, through old glass so warped and sagging the scene is dreamlike. It causes me to wonder what it was like to be a Russian on this farflung coast in the 1820s, watching a Pacific storm through windows that make the world watery and surreal.

The photos alone, however, do not convey the full vision of this book. It is the ingenious pairing of photos with quotations that span four hundred years of Bay Area life — from a Miwok legend of Coyote-man to Malvina Reynolds's satiric "Little boxes on the hillside," from the journals of the chaplain who sailed with Francis Drake to a poem by Golden Gate Bridge designer Joseph Strauss.

Accompanied by this chorus of voices, past and present, the photographs convey the same four hundred years of transformation. But it is important to bear in mind that the photos are all recent. The images depicted are all within view today, as part of the world we inhabit now. They reawaken me to the fact that these many layers of time are still with us; they coexist in the landscape and in the architecture, and in the collective experience of the region.

Kennard has found his own way to bear witness to this history. For me, his mosaic of photos and well-chosen quotes has an effect similar to that of the testimony by the oldest man at the courthouse hearing. It is both an affectionate embrace and an appeal to conscience. It reminds us how quickly things can be lost forever in the headlong rush of runaway change. It also reminds us how much still remains to be honored and preserved and attended to.

As for that subdivision, the one Ransom Rideout spoke against, it didn't happen. Many others did, of course. Since 1970 the California county I inhabit now has more than doubled in population. But those terrace lands, so far, continue to be part of the soul-stirring scenery along Highway 1. I like to think the passion of his testimony made a difference, had an effect in the unending debate about what counts most and what shape the future can take and how we are to maintain some livable balance between the relentless pressure for growth and the natural blessings that continue to draw us and hold us here.

James D. Houston, Santa Cruz, April 1987

Introduction

Crystal clear water ran out of the grassy hillside, along a carved stone channel and into an old iron basin, where it circled a few times before slipping over the edge to gather behind our dam. My younger brother David and I had cut turf nearby and built this earthen wall, topped by lush grass and buttercups as high as our knees. We watched and waited for the water to rise, but before the reservoir was filled, the ponies came down to drink and walked obliviously right through our wall, releasing a silvery rush of spring water.

On other days, we waded in the stream below the birch coppice, looking for bullheads. Blocking out the bright glare of the sky with our bodies, we slowly lifted stones from the sandy bottom and searched for the camouflaged shapes of the ugly little fish. Our noses to the water, we watched our magnified pink hands slide up to the prey, which disappeared in a swirl of sand.

This small world of my childhood lay by the Windrush, a tributary of the River Thames, in the Cotswold Hills of western England. As I grew older, my world widened to encompass the dyer's cottage straddling the Windrush downstream. Here, it was said, cardinals' robes were dyed in earlier days; now the plump spinster Miss Tidmarsh lived here with her geese. Up in the fields, prattling old Ivor showed me the traditional way of repairing stone walls that had been pushed over by cattle or the swelling trunk of a hawthorn. Weekly I visited my grandfather's house, set at the center of three stately avenues of beech and linden trees, and it was on one of these that farmworker Leonard's older brother had carved his initials, "J. H. 1894." Leonard told me of the days when powerful shire horses pulled hay-carts up the back drive and into the dusty yard where, above the roof, the century-old wooden clocktower still stands.

Guiting Grange

River Windrush

Farther afield, outside the valley, other places made their impressions. At the foot of the hills' escarpment stood a stone arcade open to the sky, once the dim cloister of Hailes Abbey, now a sheep pasture. In the shelter of Chedworth Woods lay flint and brick mosaics depicting the four seasons, the floor of a Roman villa. At the top of a hill was the green mound of Belas Knap, a five-thousand-year-old burial site. These places each gave their character to a corner of the countryside I knew, and by their proximity placed me in a line of tradition reaching back into the distant past.

Rollright Stones, Oxfordshire

I left home for architectural school in the north, at New-castle-upon-Tyne, and later moved south again to work as a pho-tographer in London, where I lived in sight of the deep waters of the Thames. Outside the Cotswolds, the natural and man-made features of my childhood, once so closely intertwined, changed perspective. Birch trees and the sweet, heavy smell of hawthorn blossom became symbols of home as I encountered them in other parts of the country, but the landmarks—the stream, dyer's cot-tage, and Hailes Abbey—stayed in the Cotswolds and lived with me only in the memory.

Newcastle-upon-Tyne

All these things were quintessentially English and were left behind when, called by romance, I came to the United States ten years ago. American cities with their apparent jumble of signs and styles were disconcerting enough. Most perplexing was the countryside. Not only was it without familiar wildlife, but more significantly, much of it seemed to lack the stamp of man's hand. Everywhere in Europe mankind's handiwork mediates between the natural world and the viewer, giving the countryside much of its meaning. Every acre of the English landscape has been worked over for a thousand years, so much so that the "nat-ural world" no longer exists there. The course of a stream, an avenue of trees, farmyard geese—all are the result of human intervention. To me, the unworked land, bare of every familiar plant or creature, was mute, incomprehensible, and forbidding. Measured by the history of mankind's impact on the land, the vast majority of the North American continent is relatively new, but its wild regions retain an ancient natural order long vanished from Europe.

Arriving in the San Francisco Bay Area, I felt compelled to find a psychological mooring in the region's human and natural history. On long walks over San Francisco's hills, peering at gar-den birds whose names neither I nor my neighbors knew, I gradu-ally familiarized myself with new surroundings. One summer my brother visited, and we took a bus across the Golden Gate Bridge to the open hills of the Marin Headlands. Walking along the cliff's edge northward toward Muir Woods, ten miles distant, we were startled by the sight of an English inn half hidden among the trees near Muir Beach. The glimpse of the black-and-white Pelican Inn momentarily transported us back to our home, but the warm breeze and smell of sagebrush brought us back to California. I later discovered that the builder of the inn was an

Englishman, and evidently he had made a home in the region by recreating a piece of his familiar world.

In histories of the area I read colorful accounts of how other newcomers had found moorings in a new land by mapping its contours, describing its creatures, and observing its inhabitants. In whatever way earlier tides of newcomers responded to the San Francisco Bay Area, those responses added to the legacy I myself discovered with my camera and in books.

The scene and the written word reinforced each other. When, two centuries ago, Spanish diarists described the usefulness of a buckeye tree or the abundance of giant salmon, they endowed these natural features of the environment with a human aspect. In this way the buckeye now evokes a range of associations equivalent to that held by the birch tree of my childhood. Writers' accounts of human creations offered interpretations of the Bay Area's landmarks just as Ivor's and Leonard's stories interpreted the Cotswolds' landmarks. Through firsthand accounts of bygone days I could, in my imagination, extend my personal history backward. In these senses, historic accounts and the associations they brought to the landmarks and the natural landscape offered a way of making this new place home.

Ring Mountain, Marin County

This book spans the four hundred and some years since pen was first put to paper in describing this shore, its inhabitants, and their works. The descriptions nearly all survive somewhere on library shelves; the monuments of earlier times frequently have been seen as standing in the way of new plans and too often no longer exist. Surviving mission adobes, gristmills, squareriggers, salt ponds, and burial grounds are tangible records of the changing relationship between humans and the Bay Area's environment and resources. The broad bay itself, an abundance of sunshine and redwood, coastal fog and heavy winter rains, a profusion of wildlife, the remoteness and beauty of the land, and a thousand other features have combined with the cultural tendencies of the different peoples who have lived in the Bay Area in a unique and dynamic fusion of the natural and human orders, whose story is told in the rural and urban landscapes.

This is the San Francisco Bay Area that we are heirs to. Its story teaches us of the continuity of life, leading from the past on into the future. If we protect and cherish reminders of the past, we not only enrich the present and the future, but are more likely to produce works of lasting value ourselves to bequeath to future generations.

On the pages of this book, writers of the past and the scenes they visited and described meet again. In the mind's eye it is as though the meetings were happening for the first time today, the years between then and now vanished. These are sites that surround us still, sites we can visit to see the same walls and rocks, wade the same creek, hear the same birds, smell the same sagebrush. It is a meeting between us and what ancient writers called the *genius loci*, the spirit of the place, timeless and immovable as the spirit that presides over the place of our childhood. ❧

Saint Bonaventure, Old Mission San Jose

The World of Coyote-man

The world was made by Coyote-man.

Indians riding a bulrush balsa on San Francisco Bay

T he myths are related by the old people after the first rains of the winter season, usually in the ceremonial roundhouse and always at night by the dim light of a small flickering fire. They constitute the religious history of the tribe, and from time immemorial have been handed down by word of mouth; from generation to generation they have been repeated, without loss and without addition." This oral tradition blended mystery, reverence, instruction, and humor in recounting the story of the creation of the world by animal gods after a cataclysmic flood and the animal gods' subsequent exploits.

Early European settlers had little patience for the many tales of wily Coyote-man, Frog-woman, and Hummingbird. Only when the tradition was brought to the verge of extinction by white man's activities did the new possessors of the land listen to the ancient native wisdom. During the last years of the nineteenth century, C. Hart Merriam, an ethnologist, recorded scores of Miwok Indian stories, later published in his rare book *Dawn of the World*; the quotation above is taken from the book's preface. Merriam wrote at a time when mythical Coyote-man's world was alive in the memory of the oldest generation of the Bay Area's native people. Another generation has since been born and buried, and Coyote-man's world and his pranks seem lost forever. Or are the frog and hummingbird incarnations of those first mythical creatures, waiting for the smoke to clear before Coyote-man makes a comeback?

The forested mountains and luxuriant valleys of California's coastal edge were inhabited long before Babylon was built, and even before the ocean rose, flooded through the Golden Gate, and formed San Francisco Bay ten thousand years ago. The

Kule Loklo Indian village, Marin County

Olompali, Marin County

natives whom Europeans encountered in the sixteenth century were the latest in a slow succession of peoples whose culture had already existed for two thousand years.

The Bay Area of those times was a very different place than it is now. Much of today's urban area was bayshore marshland teeming with waterfowl; the valleys and foothills were studded with food-bearing oaks and were home to antelope, elk, deer, and bear; the hills on both sides of the bay were clothed with towering redwood forests spreading down to valley floors, and there hazelnuts and berries could be found. Today, anyone who attempted to rely on indigenous plants and animals would soon starve to death.

Rodeo Beach, Marin County

Bay Area natives lived on the bountiful natural produce of the land without the need of either agriculture or the nomadic life common in other parts of the continent. The closest they came to crop raising was to burn over grassland to promote useful seed-producers. By careful observation of the natural world they could fulfill their needs with a rudimentary technology. From stone they fashioned sharp arrowpoints, from herbs came rope, and by patiently learning the habits of their prey they kept hunger away. Most necessary supplies could be obtained within a few square miles of hill, valley, and shoreline. What could not readily be found was traded: salt for obsidian, salmon for beads.

Daily life was a perpetual round of gathering and processing food and making the tools necessary for these activities. Routines and diet varied according to the season: ducks were plentiful in winter, salmon in spring, seeds in summer; acorns, the year-round staple, were collected in the fall. Careful planning and painstaking work were required to provide for a family's needs throughout the year. The population was stable and peaceable, and their artifacts and refuse were impermanent or harmless to the environment. Most probably their way of life could have continued indefinitely had not outsiders interfered.

To the Indians, the material world was closely shadowed by a spiritual world—or perhaps vice versa. Spirits lived in creeks, trees, and many other features of the landscape and could be re-assuring and benevolent, or vengeful if treated with disrespect. The result was a very conservative attitude toward change in the environment and a reluctance to travel outside home territory.

Abundance of food in the Bay Area allowed the population to exist in small groups socially, politically, and even linguistically independent of each other. Territories generally straddled a watercourse, the main axis of daily life, and joined on ridgetops, where food was scarcer.

At the time of Spanish settlement in 1776, about twenty thousand Indians lived in the seven thousand square miles now comprising the nine San Francisco Bay Area counties. Just sixty-five years of European contact reduced the native population to a bewildered few, their traditional way of life torn to shreds. ❧

Digger pine cone, eight inches long

Coast redwoods

Pomo carrying basket

The world was made by O-ye the Coyote-man. The earth was covered with water. The only thing that showed above the water was the very top of Oonnahpis.

In the beginning O-ye came on a raft from the west from across the ocean. His raft was a mat of tules and split sticks; it was long and narrow. O-ye landed on the top of Oonnahpis and threw his raft-mat out over the water—the long way north and south, the narrow way east and west; the middle rested on the rock on top of the peak. This was the beginning of the world and the world is still long and narrow like the mat. . . .

When O-ye was sitting alone on top of Oonnahpis, and all the rest of the world was covered with water, he saw a feather floating toward him, blown by the wind from the west—the direction from which he himself had come. He asked the feather, "Who are you?"

A cirrus cloud hangs like Hooloope the Hummingbird, bringer of light to the world, over flat-topped Oonnahpis—Sonoma Mountain—in Coast Miwok mythology the site of Creation. To the Miwok people the natural world, human beings, and the land they inhabited were inextricably bound together. Coyote-man and his

family, apparently animals yet behaving like humans, created the human world. The Creator first planted trees useful to humans: the buckeye, source of fire-making drills; the elderberry, for its edible blue fruit; and the oak, for its abundant crop of acorns, once the staple food of Bay Area Indians.

The feather made no reply.

He then told the feather about his family and all his relatives. When he came to mention Wekwek, his grandson, the feather leaped up out of the water and said, "I am Wekwek, your grandson!"

O-ye the Coyote-man was glad, and they talked together.

Every day O-ye noticed Kotolah the Frog-woman sitting near him. Every time he saw her he reached out his hand and tried to catch her, but she always jumped into the water and escaped.

After four days the water began to go down, leaving more land on top of the mountain, so that Kotolah had to make several leaps to reach the water. This gave O-ye the advantage and he ran after her and caught her. When he had caught her he was surprised to find she was his own wife from over the ocean. Then he was glad.

When the water went down and the land was dry O-ye planted the buckeye and elderberry and oak trees, and all the other kinds of trees, and also bushes and grasses, all at the same time. —*Coast Miwok*

Coyote-man . . . gathered a lot of sticks of different kinds—
some hard, as oak, madrone, and manzanita; some soft
and hollow, as the sage-herb—and made a big pile of
them and said that by and by they would turn into people.

Then he went all over the country and wherever he wanted
a village he laid down two sticks, and gave the place a name—
and the name he gave it then has always been its name and is its
name to this day. Then he went away.

In a short time the sticks turned into people, and all the
rancherias were started with the first real people.

In places where he had put sticks of hardwood the people
were strong and well and warm-blooded and could stand cold
weather; but in places where he put poor wood the people were
weak and sickly and could not stand cold weather. —*Coast Miwok*

An ancient oak frames Mount Tamalpais, at whose foot once thrived two Coast Miwok villages. The tribe's presence lingers also in the town names of Tomales and Petaluma. Bodega Bay Miwok Indian mythology cites white man's oppression as the final blow to the Indians' already sickly constitutions, inherited from the tribe's mythical ancestor, the soft-wooded sagebrush of the fog-shrouded coastal hills.

Wekwek the Falcon-man and O-lanah the Coyote-man lived a long time ago. Wekwek did not like O-lanah because he was smart and always pretended that he could do everything. So one day Wekwek said to him, "Let's go and get wood; you are so smart and know so much and can do so many things, let's see you take that big oak tree and bring it home."

O-lanah answered, "All right, I can do it."

Wekwek told him to go ahead and do it.

Then O-lanah ran around and around the big oak tree and the roots cracked and made a noise, and the tree shook, but it did not fall; O-lanah could not get it up; he made it shake four times but could not make it fall.

Wekwek, who was watching from the top of a sycamore tree, said, "Do that again; make the big oak tree shake again, the same as you did before, you are so strong."

The valley oak (*Quercus lobata*), one of the largest of North American oaks, was once commonly found alongside the river channels of the Delta region, home of Miwok Indians. Other denizens of the valley were the prairie falcon and coyote (pictured here), but the original habitat and its wildlife have all but disappeared under pressure

from agriculture. Coyotes still roam at night in the Bay Area's uplands, where they prey on small mammals, birds, and reptiles. Livestock owners regard coyotes as pests, but in spite of year-round hunting to control the population and collect the valued pelts, the canny animals continue to increase in numbers.

O-lanah tried but could not do it.

Then Wekwek said, "What you said was not true; you bragged that you could do everything but you cannot do anything; now I have beaten you, haven't I?"

"Yes," answered O-lanah, "You have beaten me; I am going away." Then O-lanah turned and howled as Coyotes howl and cried and said "*how-loo-loo-e, how-loo-loo-e, how-loo-loo-e,*" and turned into a real Coyote like the coyotes we have now." —*Miwok*

They are people of a tractable, free, and loving nature, without guile or treachery; their bowes and arrowes (their only weapons, and almost all their wealth) they use very skillfully, but yet not to do any great harm with them, being by reason of their weakenesse, more fit for children then for men, sending the arrow neither farre off, nor with any great force; and yet are the men commonly so strong of body, that that which two or three of our men could hardly beare, one of them would take upon his backe, and without grudging, carrie it easily away, up hill and downe hill an English mile together; they are also exceeding swift in running, and of long continuance. . . . One thing we observed in them with admiration: that if at any time they chanced to see a fish so neere the shoare that they might reach the place without swimming, they would never, or very seldome misse to take it. —*Francis Fletcher 1579*

The tracks of four animals cross on the beach at Point Reyes: the distinct pads of a raccoon, a bounding jack rabbit, a walking mule deer passing right to left, and more faintly, a gray fox. Dimples in the sand tell of earlier travelers who passed by before the tide rose and fell.

Many moons ago, Francis Drake's chaplain, Francis Fletcher, landed at the same bay and penned a vignette of the land's natives. The Indians are long gone, but their spirits seem to persist in the animals that populated their myths and still run free.

The greatest mechanical ingenuity displayed by the Indians is in the construction of their baskets and bows and arrows. Some of the former constructed of the barks of trees are water-tight and used for carrying water. . . . Many of the baskets are ornamented with the scarlet feathers of the *Oriolus phoeniceus* or with the black crest feathers of the Californian partridge, and are really very handsome. The Californian bow is of a good shape, from three feet to four feet and a half long, neatly wrought and strengthened with the tendons of deer. . . . The arrows, as well as the bows, are neatly wrought having points of obsidian or a kind of flint, which are let into the wood and bound fast with tendons. — *Alexander Forbes 1830s*

Pomo Indian baskets took weeks of skillful handiwork to create, and are amongst the finest on the continent. The one here was formed from a coil of willow branch laced with sedge root and decorated with beads and quail crest-feathers; red woodpecker feathers once attached have worn off. The few basketmakers of today carefully guard the whereabouts of their source materials, which have become scarce owing to land drainage and grazing. One plot of

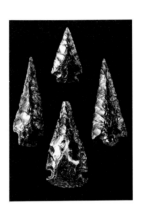

sedge plants in Sonoma County—home of the Pomo—was transplanted by the Army Corps of Engineers to save it from being destroyed by the construction of a dam. Arrowpoints were most commonly of obsidian, a black volcanic glass mined at Glass Mountain near Saint Helena and at other sites in the North Bay and traded around the Bay Area. After the arrival of glass bottles for medicine and drink, glass itself was chipped into beautiful and razor-sharp points.

W̱e have noted that the fish most abundant at present from the mouth of the bay to here are the salmon. They are very red in color, and are tender, and none of those we have seen is less than five quarters long. Today we met twenty-two heathen loaded with these fish and from carrying four apiece they werre almost bushed. At the village which we passed there were so many that it seems impossible that its residents could eat them, and yet part of the inhabitants were in their little tule rafts engaged in catching more. —*Juan Bautista de Anza 1776*

Bay Area Indians caught the magnificent king salmon with spears, harpoons, traps, and in open water, with staked nets. A line and hook of thorn or bone was used for smaller fish. Early Spanish explorer Juan Bautista de Anza's diary entry for April 3, 1776, describes salmon over three and a half feet long caught in Suisun Bay. After plentiful catches, the salmon meat could be stored sun-dried or baked and pulverized for later use. Today, although the salmon's natural spawning grounds have been greatly reduced by siltation and the building of dams and levees, there is still a considerable run of twenty- to forty-pound fish up the Sacramento River.

The Indian deer-hunter's aim for the heart was so sure that his shy prey, patiently stalked through grassland or brush, dropped dead with the flight of an arrow without being able to warn the herd. The muffled bowstring did not betray the hunter's presence, and thus several animals could be killed in a single foray. The skill of hunting with the bow and arrow almost died with the last wild Indian of California early this century but is now popular with hunter-hobbyists. Mule deer, guarded by a long closed season and without natural predators apart from the uncommon mountain lion, are plentiful to the point of being a menace to suburban gardens.

W̱e saw an Indian with a stag's head fixed upon his own walk on all fours, as if he were browsing the grass, and he played this pantomime to such perfection that all our hunters would have fired at him at thirty paces had they not been prevented; in this manner they approach herds . . . within a very small distance, and kill them with a flight of arrows. —*Jean François de Galaup, Comte de La Pérouse 1786*

The acorns of all three species of oak, the live oak, oak, and the cork tree, are all used to make *atole* and *pinole*; the acorns are treated in this manner: After they have been skinned and dried in the sun, they are beaten in stone mortars . . . until they are reduced to a powder or flour. This is mixed with a suitable quantity of water in close-woven baskets, washed repeatedly, and the sediment or coarse flour allowed to settle. This done, it is now put on the sand and sprinkled with more water until the mass begins to harden and break up, and becomes filled with cracks. It is now ready to eat, uncooked, and is called *pinole* or bread. A part may be boiled in a suitable quantity of water, when it is called *atole* or gruel. — *Pedro Fages 1775*

The months of October and November were acorn-gathering time. Tanbark oak acorns, shown here, were preferred because of their large size and imperviousness to insects. Indian names for seasons were evocative of weather and work, as in "pattering showers" and "bear-hunting time." Apparently the native people took little note of passing years and generations.

Depressions in boulders and bedrock served as mortars where womenfolk passed endless hours grinding acorns. With each generation the cavities went deeper into the rock. The mortar rock opposite is now surrounded by Berkeley's homes and gardens. Four types of acorn were eaten: valley oak ("oak"), coast live oak, black oak, and tanbark oak (called "cork tree" from its resemblance to *Quercus suber*). Several washings of the flour were necessary to remove the bitter and poisonous tannin. To make gruel, flour and water were placed in a tightly woven basket; hot rocks were then dropped inside to cook the meal.

The Indians distinguish the seasons of the year by means of phases of the moon, rains, cold, heat, and especially by the season for gathering seeds, and above all by the season for gathering acorns for these form their principle sustenance. They have no other calendars but these. The regulation of the hours of the day is determined by the rising and setting of the sun on the visible horizon. — *Fathers Narciso Durán and Buenaventura Fortuny 1814*

W̶e saw a large storehouse on shore. . . . We landed, and found ourselves *above* an Indian village, for here they live underground, and we could hear their voices beneath us. Several old women and children made their appearance; we gave them some beads. —*Peter Corney 1814*

Coast Miwok Indian builders sunk their halls at least halfway into the ground and covered them over with logs, brush, and soil. These construction techniques provided insulation from heat and cold, and by reducing wall height, made the structures more stable. This dance house at Kule Loklo on Point Reyes National Seashore was constructed using traditional techniques and with the blessing of descendants of the Coast Miwok. Ritual and healing ceremonies are again performed in the ancient setting.

The Point Reyes Peninsula was the departure point for the ghosts of the Nicasio and Tomales Bay Indians. Periodically villagers celebrated the return of the ghosts, and it has been said that the coincidence of Francis Drake's arrival in Marin with an occasion of the ghosts' return accounts for the reverential treatment he was given. Pictured opposite is the Santa Maria Valley on the Point Reyes National Seashore.

W̶hen a person dies his Walle or Ghost goes to Helwah the West, crossing the great ocean to Ootayome, the Village of the Dead. In making this long journey it follows *hinnan mooka,* the path of the Wind. Sometimes Ghosts come back and dance in the roundhouse; sometimes people hear them dancing inside but never see them. —*Coast Miwok*

This Kingdome

*By the grace of God in the name of Herr Majesty Queen Elizabeth of England
and herr successors forever, I take possession of this kingdome.*

*Drake welcomed by Coast Miwok Indians
(depicted as East Coast natives)*

*Map of California coastline
drawn by Miguel Costansó, 1770*

The discovery of the vast expanse of the Pacific Ocean by Europeans in 1513 was a great setback for international trade. Spain was looking for a western route to the Orient and in crossing the Isthmus of Panama had stumbled on the truth that a separate continent and another ocean lay between the Atlantic and Asia. But it was not long before Spanish *conquistadores* had found Central and South America's wealth in gold and were exploring up the fogbound Pacific coast. In 1542, in a symbolic gesture, Juan Rodríguez Cabrillo claimed California for Spain.

Nearly four decades later Francis Drake landed on the lush Marin coast to repair his ship, and he likewise claimed California for his monarch, the Queen of England. Following this visit of 1579, California lay blissfully ignored for nearly two hundred years, except for occasional reprovisioning forays by Spanish galleons returning laden with silk and spices from Manila.

By the second half of the eighteenth century imperial competition, hastened by improved navigational techniques, had become more heated in the northern Pacific. Russians were hunting in Alaskan coastal waters; Britain was searching for a sea passage over North America to open an Oriental trade route avoiding Spanish-controlled areas; Spain, already well established in Mexico, urged that colony to substantiate against other European powers the royal claim on the virtually unknown region northward to Monterey Bay and Point Reyes. So it was that the Bay Area eventually became a part of the kingdom of Spain, a rule that was to last until Mexican (and with it Californian) independence in 1821.

Short of colonists in the New World, Spain realized that it needed the loyalty and labor of whatever natives inhabited

*Mount Tamalpais State Park,
Marin County*

Map based on José Cañizares' survey of 1775

Bull elk

California and entrusted the control and training of them to Catholic missionaries. Small military forces were sent to protect the friars and warn off foreign intruders. In 1769 land and sea expeditions set out northward from Baja California; after the founding of a fort and mission at San Diego Bay, a party of indomitable trailblazers led by Gaspar de Portolá scrambled up through the coastal mountains but missed their goal—Monterey Bay—and found themselves looking down on a broad arm of the sea, later named San Francisco Bay.

These soldiers, together with the Franciscan friar Father Juan Crespí, spent nearly five and a half months traveling more than thirteen hundred miles over unmapped, often trackless and inhospitable terrain; members of other exploring parties sent to California died from privations. Yet rarely are expressions of the extreme sufferings that the early soldiers, friars, and colonists endured found in their diaries. Part of the explanation is that the diaries were written to become official reports on the lay of the land, its natives, and the industriousness of the explorers themselves. But the explorers were also strengthened by a staunch loyalty to their king, and by a fervent faith in God's intent to save the country's heathen souls from damnation.

As it turned out, colonization of the Bay Area under Spanish rule achieved little. A crude military *presidio* was built in 1776 at the Golden Gate, and for forty-six years the Spanish flag fluttered over it, threatening war against trespassers. The sheltered anchorage was a valuable strategic asset, but neither the five missions' farms nor the tiny civilian *pueblo* of San José at the south end of the bay produced much wealth for the mother country.

Neither did the few hundred Spaniards, gathered in mud-walled settlements smaller than many of the native villages, in their time make much impression on the Bay Area's landscape. They had arrived with just a handful of horses, cattle, and agricultural supplies. However, they sowed the seeds—literally and metaphorically—that were to radically alter the environment and the lives of its first inhabitants. ❧

Inscription on Spanish cannon

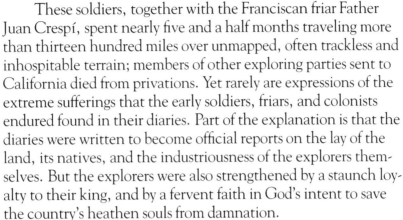

Gaspar de Portolá's signature

T his country our generall named *Albion*, and that for two causes: the one in respect of the white bancks and cliffes, which lie toward the sea; the other, that it might have some affinity even in name also, with our owne country, which was sometime so called. — *Francis Fletcher 1579*

The pale cliffs of what is now Drake's Bay on the Point Reyes National Seashore, opposite, reminded Francis Drake of the white cliffs of Dover in his native England. According to the account of his chaplain, Francis Fletcher, they inspired him to name the land Albion—a name the Romans had given England (*albus* meaning "white" in Latin). Landing here in 1579, Drake stayed for five weeks while his crew repaired the ship before continuing the westward journey to Europe.

Olema Valley, seen here from Inverness Ridge on the Point Reyes National Seashore, divides the Point Reyes Peninsula from the rest of Marin County. The San Andreas fault follows the line of the valley, and motion along the fault continues to shift Point Reyes in a northwesterly direction. Since Drake's visit, the western side of Olema Valley may have crept as much as seventy feet to the northwest. Movement over millions of years has carried the uncharacteristic granite land mass of the peninsula hundreds of miles from where it was formed.

O ur generall with his gentlemen, and many of his company, made a journey up into the land, to see the manner of [the inhabitants'] dwellings, and to be better acquainted with the nature and commodities of the country. . . . The inland we found to be farre different from the shoare, a goodly country, and fruitfull soyle, stored with many blessings fit for the use of man; infinite was the company of very large and fat Deere, which we saw by the thousands. — *Francis Fletcher 1579*

Friday, the 26th., dawned with the sky overcast, and the fog was so thick that at the distance of a musket-shot nothing could be seen. About four o'clock in the morning the wind which we had had during the night shifted to the west-northwest, and the ship's head was put to east-southeast. This morning we saw many birds, both great and small, and ducks and many whales, not very far away from the ship. All this indicates that we are not very far from the coast. . . .

At about nine o'clock, it began to blow very strong from the northwest. About ten o'clock it was said that land was in sight on the bow and not very distant, although I was able to make it out with difficulty because of the thick fog. The Captain said that these were the *farallones* of San Francisco. . . .

The first group, which we saw very plainly as we passed it about a league away, is that toward the north, and consists of seven small rocky crags, not very large nor equal in size. . . . In order to pass by them the ship's head was put south by east. By mid-day they were astern, and had there been a clear sun, this would have been a good opportunity for the determination of their latitude. At this same hour of noon we began to make out the second group. They also are seven in number, and are very lofty. They seemed to be contiguous, and seen from afar, appeared to form an island with seven peaks, some higher than others, with a circumference of about a league. Of these, it would appear, Admiral Cabrera Bueno speaks, when he says that that they make a good landmark for finding Port San Francisco.
—*Father Juan Crespí 1774*

The Farallon Islands, scattered over eight miles of ocean thirty miles west from the mouth of San Francisco Bay, were discovered by Spanish ships more than two centuries before the bay itself was discovered. Coastal fog and the blending of landforms had effectively concealed the bay's entrance. Francis Drake restocked with seal and seabird meat taken from the islands, which he named Saint James. In 1774, when the Spanish ship *Santiago* came within a league (three miles) of the islands, the ship's diarist, Father Juan Crespí, referred to them as the Farallones (a Spanish nautical term meaning rocky islets), but it is not known who so named them. Today the Farallones constitute the Farallon National Wildlife Refuge, protecting seabirds, elephant seals (pictured here), and sea lions. In the absence of predation by land animals—and the general public—over a quarter of a million birds, including common murres, western gulls (nest shown here), Cassin's auklets, and cormorants, nest on the islands. On clear days in winter and spring the Southeast Farallon can be espied from coastal cliffs as little pinnacles on the western horizon.

We went on for a league more to the northwest and halted on the bank of an *arroyo* which is about one league from the parallel of the gate. As soon as we stopped the soldiers succeeded in killing a bear, so that they had fresh meat to go on with. In the march of this day we came to seven *arroyos* of running water; three of them are opposite the gate, spread over the plain, and empty into the estuary. On the plain we saw many lilies and an abundance of very leafy sweet marjoram. — *Father Juan Crespí 1772*

Strawberry Creek, here edged by redwoods and the twisted trunk of a buckeye, runs through the Berkeley campus of the University of California. In 1772, when a dozen soldiers accompanied by Father Crespí rested at what was most likely this very creek, California grizzlies abounded in the area, and irises and coyote-mint too (if these are Crespí's "lilies and sweet marjoram"). The plants still grow in untended spots in Oakland and Berkeley, but the state's grizzly was hunted to extinction by 1924.

November 28. The day broke very clear, and before sunrise we saw a rainbow in the west. About seven we set out from the camping place in a northwesterly direction, following the same plain. The day's march, although it has not been more than four hours and a half, has been very heavy, for although it has been all over level ground, yet it has been troublesome on account of the thick groves of junipers and madrones . . . although the woods were interspersed with good spots of land covered with grass, oaks and live-oaks. —*Father Francisco Palóu 1774*

Manzanita is a formidable barrier to foot travel and sometimes grows as high as fifteen feet. Searching for a suitable site for a mission at the port of San Francisco, a party of Spanish trailblazers led by Captain Fernando Rivera y Moncada battled through such brush near what is now Cupertino, as recorded by Father Francisco Palóu. Palóu mentioned "junipers and madrones" but must have been describing chamise or coyotebrush and manzanita, whose smooth reddish bark resembles that of the madrone, an open-forest tree.

We traveled . . . for another three and a half leagues, through very charming country, more thickly grown with redwoods, live oaks, and oaks loaded with acorns. Two numerous villages of heathen came to meet us with demonstrations of great pleasure, bringing us a good present of *pinole*, black *tamales*, and porridge made of acorns, which relieved in part the hunger of the men, who were reduced . . . to only five *tortillas* a day. —*Father Juan Crespí 1769*

The coppices and plains are full of little grey crested partridges, which, like those of Europe, flock together but in covies of three or four hundred. They are fat, and very well flavored. The trees are the habitation of the most charming birds, and our ornithologists stuffed many varieties. —*Jean François de Galaup, Comte de La Pérouse 1786*

Indians made a kind of *tamale* or dumpling from the seed of the holly-leaf cherry (pictured), a plant that lends its Indian name, *islais*, to a creek in San Francisco. Gaspar de Portolá was leading an expedition of about sixty men, including Father Crespí, in a vain search for Monterey Harbor, and the soldiers were starving. In the neighborhood of Woodside in San Mateo County they assuaged their hunger with foods brought to them by natives. The following day the soldiers ate acorns they collected themselves, and not knowing how to prepare the food, became violently sick. On the return journey south, hunger drove them to eating a mule a day.

Early scientists encountered a wealth of new discoveries in the Bay Area, including the California quail. After Drake, the first non-Hispanic foreigner to set foot in California was the head of a French scientific and geographic expedition, Comte de La Pérouse. The California quail was to proliferate with the introduction of cattle ranching due to a favorable relationship of the bird's feeding ground to brush cover brought about by grazing. However it later suffered from commercial hunting by Americans until its sale was outlawed at the beginning of this century. Now the state bird, the quail is common wherever brush and water are close, and is considered fair game by sports hunters both in its home state and in Nevada and Oregon, where it was introduced a hundred years ago.

W hile exploring in this place some bands of animals were seen which must have numbered more than fifty, accompanied by their young. They were as large as cows, without horns, the color of deer, with feet like cows, head and face like mules, and the excrement the same. — *Father Juan Crespi 1770*

Elk were once numerous in all parts of the Bay Area, but in a hundred years they were hunted to the verge of extinction. From a handful in Kern County, tule elk have been nursed back to a count of about seven hundred animals in a dozen herds. In the Bay Area they are seen again at Point Reyes (where the photograph was taken), on Grizzly Island in Suisun Bay, and around the hills of the Concord Naval Weapons Station.

All this bay, which is called "the round bay" (though it is not so), is bordered by rough hill country without trees except for woodlands in the two coves to the southwest; the rest is barren, irregular, and of melancholy aspect. Aside from the channels, in no part of it is the depth more than five cubits; at low tide it is two and half and some parts are dry. Getting into it is not difficult, but getting out is otherwise, for we found that the prevailing winds are from the southwest. Although I searched its shores with close attention, I found no fresh water. —*José Cañizares 1775*

San Pablo Bay, here seen beneath the limbs of a live oak on the bay's western side, was first surveyed in 1775 by José Cañizares, sailing master of the ship *San Carlos*, the earliest vessel to sail into San Francisco Bay. Cañizares searched the shores in vain for a water source that was not made brackish by tidal movement, as are the Petaluma and Napa rivers and San Pablo Creek. Today San Pablo Bay is considerably smaller and shallower, owing to extensive diking, filling, and siltation over the past 150 years.

W̲e arrived at the *arroyo* of San Francisco, on whose banks is the redwood which I mentioned yesterday. I measured its height with a graphometer which they loaned me at the Mission San Carlos del Carmelo, and found it to be, according to the calculation which I made, some fifty *varas* high, a little more or less. The trunk at the foot was five and a half *varas* in circumference. — *Father Pedro Font 1776*

The ancient coast redwood still standing by San Francisquito Creek in Palo Alto ("tall tree" in Spanish) is generally assumed to be the one measured by Franciscan friar Pedro Font in 1776. Using a surveying instrument, Font calculated its height as about 140 feet. From the time of its discovery in 1770, it long served as a landmark for travelers and later became a Mexican ranch boundary marker. Still later a farm was named after it, and after the farm, the town of Palo Alto.

All that survives of San Francisco's Spanish Presidio is a few durable cannon barrels and an adobe wall encased in the present-day Officers' Club. Seen here is the bronze barrel of the cannon *San Pedro*, cast in Peru in 1673, and crudely emblazoned with the arms of Spain. The Presidio's founding in 1776 was recorded by the friar Francisco Palóu, who celebrated the first masses at both this site and that selected for Mission Dolores. A continent away, the ink was scarcely dry on the Declaration of Independence for thirteen American colonies. The eighty-five-square-yard Spanish Presidio was never adequately maintained, and its adobe buildings and fortifications were ruins by 1840. Today the Presidio is headquarters for the United States Sixth Army, and its once bare hills lie under a towering forest of century-old eucalyptus and cypress.

A̲s soon as the bark was made fast, the commander, pilots, and Father Nocedal went ashore. When they saw the site of the camp they were all of the opinion that it was a very suitable place for the fort and *presidio*, and they thought the same of the site of the Laguna de los Dolores for the mission. In view of the opinion of the captain of the bark and the pilots, work was begun on the building of the houses and the *presidio*. A square measuring ninety-two *varas* each way was marked out for it, with divisions for church, royal offices, warehouses, guard-house, and houses for soldier settlers, a map of the plan being formed and drawn by the first pilot.

And so that the work might be done as speedily as possible, the commander designated a squad of sailors and the two carpenters to join the servants of the royal *presidio* in making a good warehouse in which to keep the provisions, a house for the commanding officer of the *presidio*, and a chapel for celebrating the holy sacrifice of the Mass, while the soldiers were making their own houses for their families. — *Father Francisco Palóu 1776*

I t gave very good water, and experience afterwards demonstrated that it was excellent and of miraculous qualities. In proof of my assertions I appeal to the families of Miramontes, Martínez, Sánchez, Soto, Briones, and others, all of whom several times had twins. —*Mariano Guadalupe Vallejo 1830s.*

The spring El Polín, running out of the side of a sandhill, supplied drinking water for the Presidio of San Francisco. Before the Spanish arrived, the spring had earned a magical reputation among the Costanoan Indians, and Mariano Guadalupe Vallejo, commander of the Presidio during the period of Mexican rule, noted that it redoubled the fertility of many soldiers' families. Other springs were located near today's Mason and Washington streets, and "Spanish Springs" was on Steiner Street. Pictured in El Polín's water is the seep-spring monkeyflower; nowadays only birds drink here, and a hummingbird comes down to bathe in the outflow.

The full moon in the early dawn light sinks toward the ocean outside the Golden Gate. Any foreigner entering San Francisco Bay risked fire from the Spanish fort, but this did not deter the Russian Count Rezanov, who in 1806 sought food for his starving compatriots in Alaska in exchange for manufactured goods. His vessel *Juno* was American-built, and his log keeper Nikolai Aleksandrovich Khvostov read an English map; the crew included Englishmen and Aleuts. Such was the cosmopolitan nature of navigation in the Pacific. Spain's attempt to bar foreigners from the thinly settled province was sound policy, but futile because the settlers were so poorly supplied by Spanish ships. Little wonder that Spain lost its grip on California—but under Mexican rule, too, California was to remain a distant and neglected province.

A t daybreak, at 4 o'clock, before the garrison of the fort could get our range, we weighed anchor, but unfortunately the tide was going out and the wind was light topgallant sail, so the ship could not make more than 3½ knots. As we learned afterward, the current at full moon was 6¼ Italian miles per hour until 10 o'clock in the morning. At 8 o'clock, when we could see the fort and many people at the embrasures, the tide began to ease, the breeze grew stronger; so we set all the studding sails and went straight into the gate. —*Nikolai Aleksandrovich Khvostov 1806*

I Am a Christian Indian

I am a Christian Indian
I am all that is left of my people.

Father Narciso Durán and an Indian child
at Mission San Jose

Spain believed that by means of the mission system of combining the provision of food and shelter with instruction in religion, agriculture, and handicrafts, the native population could be made a dependent and useful workforce. It is astonishing that the instruments of this plan were a small group of Franciscan friars (usually there were two *padres* at each mission) directed by a superior in the Church and backed up by an undisciplined band of soldiers. More astonishing is the fact that the plan might have succeeded had foreign diseases not struck down the natives.

Sanctus bell wheel, Old Mission
San Jose

The friars' aims were to bring heathen souls into the Christian God's fold and to train the Indians in civilized occupations. To these ends they divided the coastal territory of California among twenty-one missions and declared the respective Indian populations their sphere of religious activity and the mountains and valleys theirs for ranching and agriculture.

Of the five missions in the Bay Area, Misión San Francisco de Asís (Mission Dolores) in San Francisco was the first founded, in 1776; in the following year, Misión Santa Clara de Asís was founded; Misión San José, in today's Fremont, followed in 1797; Misión San Rafael Arcángel, in 1817; and last and most northerly in California, Misión San Francisco Solano in Sonoma, in 1823.

Ceiling of Mission Dolores,
painted by natives

Indians were initially tempted to the mission compounds by curiosity, food, and novel clothing, but once enrolled, soldiers ensured their continued attendance. Some five to six thousand Indians lived at the five missions in the early 1800s. The tribes were mixed indiscriminately, multiplying the friars' language problems. Mission Indians took a reluctant part in the genesis of agriculture in the Bay Area, with varying degrees of success—whether measured in yield or educational value.

In the space of a few years, the age-old way of life in the Bay Area was upset. Familial relationships were shattered, religious artifacts destroyed, and traditional food-gathering activities disturbed by the new overlords. Livestock grazed where seeds had been gathered yearly; wildlife became more timorous and difficult to hunt; and much land simply became off-limits to any Indian who valued his independence. Only north of Bodega Bay were the natives beyond the influence of the missions.

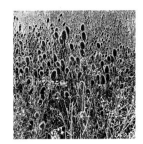

Fuller's teasel, introduced by the Spanish

The friars were selfless, devout men, willing to give their lives for their beliefs, but they carried the white man's burden, common to their time, of feeling obliged to lead others in a Christian pattern of life and belief. In other colonies, secular authorities had been assigned the training of natives, and the results were disastrous when the keepers sought to enrich themselves at the expense of the Indians. In California, mission Indians received relatively mild treatment and were naturally amenable.

Medicine phials, Old Mission San Jose

Christianity did prevail over native customs, but not by the means intended. With white men—both Hispanics and other foreigners, trappers, and traders—came diseases fatal to the natives. Attacks of smallpox, measles, diphtheria, and malaria wiped out two-thirds of California's Indian population by the mid-1830s. At the missions syphilis, abortion, and infanticide further reduced a demoralized population. An American census of the Bay Area in 1860 recorded just 871 Indians.

Not only disease but also governmental neglect sent the missions into decline. In 1821 California came under the rule of an independent Mexico, and the new government was more interested in dividing up the land and encouraging Mexican settlers than in coaching Indians. In 1833–36 the missions were secularized: the Catholic Church's virtually monopolistic authority over land was abolished, and the mission sanctuaries were reduced to the status of parish churches. Without a land base, the friars could no longer support an Indian population, whose survivors dispersed among the newly formed Mexican *ranchos* as farmhands and servants.

Title page of baptismal register of Sonoma Mission

San Juan Capistrano, Mission Dolores

Of the original Bay Area mission buildings little survives. Built of sun-dried bricks, they were very vulnerable to weather damage; with a few years of neglect, or an earthquake or fire, they were reduced to mudheaps. Today all the mission sites are commemorated by churches, but only Mission Dolores has an original Spanish sanctuary. Old Mission San Jose has recently added a reconstructed adobe church to its original mission quarters, and Sonoma has an atmospheric arcade and courtyard, in one corner of which is a simple chapel built in Mexican times. ❧

I came to a large rock with a cleft in the middle of it, in which rested three remarkable droll objects, and I was led to wonder if they were likenesses of some idol that the Indians reverenced.

These were slim round shafts about a yard and half high, ornamented at the top with bunches of white feathers, and ending, to finish them off, in an arrangement of black and red-dyed feathers imitating the appearance of a sun. They even had, as their drollest adornment, pieces of the little nets with which we had seen the Indians cover their hair.

At the foot of this niche were many arrows with their tips stuck in the ground as if symbolizing abasement. This last exhibit gave me the unhappy suspicion that those bunches of feathers representing the image of the sun . . . must be objects of the Indians' heathenish veneration; and if this was true—as was a not unreasonable conjecture—these objects suffered a merited penalty in being thrown on the fire. —*Father Vicente Santa María 1775*

Nuestra Señora de los Angeles ("Our Lady of the Angels") was the name Juan Manuel de Ayala, captain of the ship *San Carlos*, gave to a wooded island in San Francisco Bay, presaging the missionary work of the Franciscans. Father Vicente Santa María, accompanying Ayala, found feathered offerings to the sun god that were typical of the Costanoan (Ohlone) Indian culture prevalent in the East Bay and on the San Francisco Peninsula—the first culture to succumb to missionary activity. Shown above is a serpentine outcrop that was probably exactly where these offerings were found, on what is today Angel Island State Park, lying close to Marin's shore.

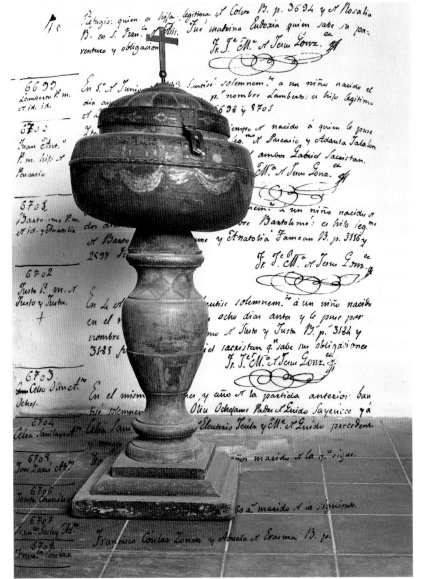

This copper and wood baptismal font was used at Mission San Jose, where over 6,500 Costanoan, Miwok, and Yokuts Indians were baptized—the highest number for any California mission. Overprinted on the photograph are records from 1833 of baptisms performed at the very same font; the signature is that of Father José María de Jesús González Rubio, a highly respected friar aged just thirty, and later to be President General over all the California missions.

On the clock striking ten we entered the church, built of stone, and neatly ornamented, where we already found some hundreds [of] half-naked Indians upon their knees, who, although they neither understand Spanish nor Latin, are not allowed to miss one mass after their conversion. . . . The confusion in the heads and hearts of these poor people, who only know how to mimick some external ceremonies, must indeed be very great. —*Otto von Kotzebue 1816*

The site chosen for San Francisco's Mission Dolores was at the edge of a lake backed by steep hills, and its second adobe church, completed in 1791, survives as the oldest building in San Francisco. The mission, as described in its twenty-fifth year by Otto von Kotzebue, a Russian navigator, consisted of the sanctuary, workshops, dormitories, and rows of dwellings for married natives. Its early agricultural activities were concentrated in the coastal valley of San Pedro, twelve miles away. After the mission closed in 1834, the San Francisco site became the scene of bullfights and bull-and-bear contests. Today, the bulls and the lake are long gone, and the dimly lit sanctuary and historic cemetery draw many hushed visitors.

Opposite: The mountains and the life they represented to mission Indians were so close yet so far from the confined life organized for them by the friars. At Mission San Jose a bell summoned Indians to service, a bell rang when meals were rationed out, and a curfew bell sent families, men, and women to their respective quarters. Compliance was enforced with the whip. Working hours were spent tilling the soil, tending cattle, or in the production of cloth, harness, soap, and candles. Sundays and thirty-four saints' days brought respite from the daily routine. Here, through an orchard's bare branches, are seen the mountains above Mission San Jose, where French artist Louis Choris observed the inhabitants in 1816.

After spending several months in the missions, they usually begin to grow fretful and thin, often casting a sad eye towards the mountains which they see in the distance. Once or twice a year, the missionaries allow those Indians they trust to return, to visit their homelands; but often, very often, few come back; however others sometimes come back with new recruits for the mission. —*Louis Choris 1816*

There are difficulties all around, and I am overburdened with cares which render life wearisome. There is hardly any of the religious in me, and I scarcely know what to do in these troublesome times. I made the vows of Friar Minor; instead I must manage temporalities, sow grain, raise sheep, horses, and cows, preach, baptize, bury the dead, visit the sick, direct carts, haul stone, lime, etc. These things are as disagreeable as thorns, bitter, hard, unbearable, and they rob me of time, tranquility, and health, both of soul and body.
—*Franciscan missionary*

The missionary's work was not only hard, but lonely too. At times he was even without a companion friar, and relationships with the soldiers of the Presidio were always strained. The friars prevailed upon visitors to instruct the Indians in any handicrafts they knew, and for agriculture the padres relied largely on old Spanish manuals. Seen here are roof timbers and rawhide lacings originally used to secure rafters at Mission San Jose.

Father Pedro showed me the buildings and surroundings of the mission, which although founded only eight years ago, are not inconsiderable in grandeur and extent. The stock of grain in the storehouses exceeded all my expectations. They contained over 2000 *fanegas* of wheat and proportionate amounts of maize, beans, barley, peas, etc. The kitchen garden is very efficiently laid out and well kept, the soil exceedingly fertile, producing abundant harvests. The fruit-trees are still small, but doing very well. Through the garden flows a rivulet, sufficient for irrigation. A vineyard was established a few years ago and is expected to prosper. The wine should be sweet, resembling Malaga. —*Georg Heinrich von Langsdorff 1806*

Four varieties of pears grown at the missions provided fruit for the summer months. The pears shown below are the harvest of a tree descended from the original trees of Mission San Rafael. Most prosperous of the missions was Mission San Jose, described in 1806 by Georg Heinrich von Langsdorff, a German naturalist and physician who traveled down San Francisco Bay in a kayak from a ship anchored off the Presidio. The mission's lands, tended by an Indian population totaling eight hundred, extended along the eastern shore, where a large acreage was set aside for wheat, and over the mountains behind to Livermore Valley. In the 1820s these lands gave summer pasture to some nine thousand mission cattle and as many sheep. Mission San Jose's produce supplied several of the missions and the Presidio— but after harvest time Indians still went out to gather their traditional foods: acorns, seeds, and holly-leaf cherries.

In the woods not immediately bordering upon the missions, the black bear has his habitation, and when food is scarce it is dangerous to pass through them alone in the dusk of the evening; but when the acorns abound there is nothing to apprehend. . . . The lion and the tiger are natives of those woods, but we never saw them; the inhabitants say they are small, and that the lion is less than the tiger, but more powerful. A large species of mountain cat is common; a polecat also is found in the woods; wolves and foxes are numerous, and the *cuiotas*, or jackals, range about the plains at night. —*Frederick Beechey 1826*

Outlying mission herds provided easy pickings for predators. The mountain lion or cougar (pictured) is still seen occasionally in the wilder regions of the Bay Area, but being currently unprotected outside parklands, its future is uncertain. Jaguars (formerly called "tigers"), once found in California, only survive in Mexico, while bobcats ("mountain cats") and coyotes ("*cuiotas*") are quite common—although secretive—in the Bay Area.

I reckoned we had made thirteen leagues from Yerba Buena when we reached the opening of a small channel meandering in the middle of a marsh covered with reeds, and into which we entered. This stream makes a thousand turns as it advances into the interior; and although from its mouth to the spot where we landed there are not more than three leagues in a straight line, we made fully double that many in following its windings.

This passage, however, could not be shortened by making it by land; for, up to the landing place, there is no solid ground: the banks of the channel are indicated only by rushes or reeds growing in the water, or at most in a kind of mud. —*Auguste Bernard Duhaut-Cilly 1827*

Travel by boat across the bay and up winding creeks was the only way to reach Sonoma and the North Bay regions, but even to South Bay destinations boat travel was more practical for missionaries and traders than roundabout horse- back rides keeping to higher and drier ground. Two missions acquired their vessels from the Russian colony at Fort Ross in Sonoma County. French trader Auguste Bernard Duhaut-Cilly left a record of his ardu- ous journey in 1827 from the anchorage at today's San Francisco to the landing for Sonoma Mission, where he was to buy deer tallow (pro- cessed fat) used in the candlemaking industry.

W e rowed or sailed all night, and arrived the next morning at Sonoma['s landing]. The Padre . . . provided us all with horses, a whole drove of which had been brought in by Indians. We journeyed ashore, saddled the horses and, after a short gallop, arrived under the hospitable roof of our good host, who refreshed us with apples and grapes from the little mission garden, until the lunch table provided us with more substantial food. —*Edward Vischer 1842*

Sonoma's Mission San Francisco Solano was a three-mile ride from the embarcadero, where, according to the artist Edward Vischer, visitors were presented with a sampling of the horses that bred so freely in the wild. The gallop was the usual pace of travel in California, and two riders and a small herd of mounts ridden in turn could cover more than a hundred miles in a day. The mission had been secularized by the time of Vischer's visit in 1842, and the chapel seen here was new, built with materials from the ruined mission church.

A t one time San Rafael controlled 200 neophytes, 3000 cattle, 500 horses and 4500 sheep, while its harvest yielded 1500 *fanegas*. Now among its ruins only 20 Indians and an Irishman named Murphy reside. The Mission lands are rich and fertile, and tobacco plants raised by a man named Ortega appear to thrive. 2000 feet of vines have been removed at the order of Commandante Vallejo and planted on his ranch at Petaluma. . . . Livestock from San Rafael have been confiscated in a similar manner. —*Eugène Duflot de Mofras 1841*

Of the original church of Mission San Rafael, nothing but the bells survive, returned from schools and homes across the state. The inscription here reads, "1830 S. RAFAEL," honoring the healing angel whose ministrations were sorely needed to revive the sickly natives sent over from Mission Dolores. The Church's intention had always been that the neophytes (or Christianized Indians) would take over the property of the missions, but sooner or later the land and animals were all stolen or inveigled from the intended beneficiaries.

I have heard my mother say that when she danced at San Jose, one man brought an owl to the dance. The second time he brought a black crow, and the third time he brought a rattlesnake.

Fidemo was the name of the man. He said, "I am going to dance my last dance with you people. Lots of sickness is coming. We are all going to die." Nobody believed him. . . .

They came up to San Francisco, then to San Rafael. All the people died of smallpox, including the man who prophesied death. —*María Copa Frías c. 1931*

Live rattlesnakes were used in a Yokuts Indian dance ceremony in which the shaman tried to protect his people from being poisoned by snakes in the coming year. Against smallpox and other diseases brought by Europeans, the natives had no defenses; the consequences were devastating.

I am very old.
My people were once around me like the sands of the shore,
Many . . . many.
They have all passed away. They have died like the grass.
They have gone to the mountains.
I do not complain,
The antelope falls with the arrow.

I had a son. I loved him.
When the palefaces came
He went away.
I do not know where he is.

I am a Christian Indian.
I am all that is left of my people.

I am alone.

—*Indian of Mission Dolores 1850*

La Yerba Buena

A vine with a small white flower, called here la yerba buena . . .
from its abundance, gives its name to an island and town in the bay.

A group of Americans in a patriotic mood
in the Mexican town of Yerba Buena on July 4, 1836

The decline and closure of the missions in the early 1830s spelled the ascendancy of private ranchholding in California. Cattle and horses multiplied freely on the unfenced range, and already the value of stock had been discovered by the mission fathers. Hides and tallow were sought by American sea captains dropping anchor in San Francisco Bay on increasingly frequent visits. Retiring soldiers wanted to benefit from the trade and petitioned a willing Mexican government for acreages as large as today's San Francisco. The country's inhabitants were few, land was plentiful, and boundaries commensurately vague. Only in two or three cases did Indians successfully apply for the stamp of approval giving them custodianship of ground their people had inhabited for thousands of years.

Mexican ranchers depended on the labor of Indians, but foreigners too were an increasingly essential part of the economy. Besides the hide and tallow traders, by 1835 a handful of enterprising Europeans and Americans had built cabins and taken up Mexican citizenship as required for landholding. A number of these settlers were deserters from whaling ships that came to San Francisco Bay to restock supplies. The immigrants provided the technology, skills, and machinery the Mexicans lacked and were less bound by trade tariffs than their hosts.

*Mount Diablo, Contra
Costa County*

Settlement at Sonoma and elsewhere in the North Bay was encouraged by the Mexican government to keep Russian communities at Fort Ross and Bodega Bay in check. The Russians, with colonies in Kamchatka and Alaska, were hunting the northern fur seal and sea otter and were moving southward. By 1812 they had a station on the Farallon Islands within sight of the entrance to San Francisco Bay. The relationship between

Mexican spur

Fort Ross, Sonoma County

Mexican coat of arms

Mexicans and Russians was marked by suspicion but was also mutually beneficial for trading. By 1840 the Russians had virtually exterminated the sea otter and with it their reason for staying in California. The next year they sold off their goods at Fort Ross and left.

Opportunists, independent of any government, turned out to be the real threat to Mexico's authority. William Richardson deserted the British ship *Orion* in 1822, and in exchange for legal residency, taught carpentry and navigation at the Presidio. The Englishman's windy campsite, set among roaming bears and coyotes at Yerba Buena Cove on the northeastern shore of the San Francisco peninsula, soon became the nucleus of an Anglo-American community of traders. Richardson operated a shipping business serving the Mexican villages and was soon appointed Captain of the Port of San Francisco. The town of Yerba Buena, founded in 1835, was governed by Mexican authority but had few Mexican residents. Jacob Primer Leese, an American trader, set up shop in 1836 and in the same year hosted a noisy party celebrating the Fourth of July. He welcomed notable Mexicans as guests at the auspicious occasion. This ramshackle settlement was the future city of San Francisco.

Foreign residents and traders were impressed by the fecundity of the California soil and climate—and by the ineffectiveness of its government. Their glowing reports spread across the United States, along with the idea that here was a rich land for the taking. The adventurer and trapper Jedediah Smith reached the San Joaquin Valley by an overland route in 1827. By 1840, migrants were striking out westward from the river Missouri, and the following year the first emigrant party scaled the forbidding Sierra Nevada. These hardened adventurers were enacting what journalists in the United States theorized about: the fulfillment of America's Manifest Destiny, the eventual domination of the continent by Anglo-Saxons. The United States government played its part, sponsoring diplomats and explorers. What immigration might eventually have achieved, war between the United States and Mexico over Texas precipitated: in July 1846, the Stars and Stripes was raised by U.S. Navy Captain John Montgomery in Yerba Buena's Portsmouth Plaza. ❧

Bale Grist Mill, Napa County

Sōr Gōor

Muiseñor mio,

Luis Peralta Sarg.to de la Comp.a del R.l Preso. de S.n Franco Y ante el superior Govno Comicionado de este Pueblo de S.n Jose de Guadalupe, Con el devido Respecto Y subordinacion q.e deve, Parece ante V. S.a... Adistancia de ocho leguas de... Rumbo al Norte o... arroyo nombrado... licarioso,... a la Playa, Por el... o cinco leguas, Cuyo citio Y terreno Pide Y suplica se le Conceda Para Poner en el un Rancho de todos sus vienes de Camp.o, Para Por ese medio hevitar la gran de Perdida Y estravio q.e de hoyos esta estrimentan do la q.e Reciva en Grave daño Y Perjuicio de su Crecida familia;

Por tanto Pide Y suplica a la Piedad benigna de V. S. se digne Concederle la Gracia q.e solicita, sifruto del superior hagrado de V. S. de lo q.e Recivira constante Gracia;

N.ro S.r G.e a V. S. m.s a.s d.e Pueblo de S.n Jose 20 de Junio de 1820. B. L. M. de V. S.

Luis Peralta

At the distance of eight leagues from the Mission of San Jose towards the north or northwest, on the coast, there is an *arroyo* named by the Fathers of the Mission, San Leandro, and from this to a little hill standing close to the beach in the same direction, and on the same coast it is four or five leagues, which tract of land I ask may be granted to me, that I may place thereon all my stock. —*Luís Peralta 1820*

In 1820, Luís Peralta applied to the Spanish governor for the territory lying between present-day San Leandro and El Cerrito ("little hill," now Albany Hill) and received 45,000 acres as a reward for nearly forty years' service in the Spanish Army. His four sons ranched the land while he remained in San José. Peralta's house (pictured opposite) once looked onto the town plaza, where scores of ground squirrels scampered away at the entry of horsemen. The house, built in about 1800, is all that remains of the *pueblo* of San José. Here Luís Peralta lived with his wife, María Loreto Alviso, who bore him seventeen children, and presumably he died in this building in 1851, at the age of ninety-two. Peralta's letter to the governor, Pablo Vicente Solá, is printed over the photograph and translated, in part, above.

The house which the claimant [José Peña] requests has not been occupied for many years, so it will be no loss to the establishment; the small number of Indians which remain cannot fill the houses which were originally built for them. —*José Ramón Estrada 1840*

At the third site of Mission Santa Clara, dedicated by Father Junípero Serra in 1781, the Church built thirty adobe and tile-roofed cottages to house Christian Indians. Overshadowed by an olive tree, just one remains, at the side of The Alameda, the old road that led from Santa Clara to the *pueblo* of San José. After the mission's demise, in 1840 José Peña, formerly an artilleryman at the Presidio of San Francisco, successfully petitioned Governor Juan Bautista Alvarado for this same cottage and lived here while teaching letters at Santa Clara. In 1851 Santa Clara College was founded by the Jesuits, and the students used some of the mission buildings for classrooms and dormitories. José Peña died the following year, but the cottage stayed in his family until 1911, when it was bought by the Santa Clara Women's Club, in whose hands it remains today.

The whole county [of Marin] is covered with . . . grants, held in large ranches, so settlers cannot come in and settle up in smaller farms. The county is owned by not over thirty men, if we except men who have small portions near the bay or near some villages. —*William Brewer 1862*

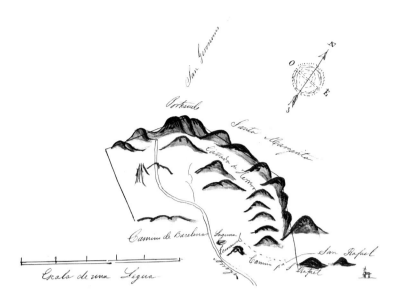

The large size of Mexican landgrants was based on the needs of cattle ranching. Americans such as William Brewer, a surveyor, saw the land in terms of its potential for cultivation. The limits of a grant were roughly established by means of a sketch, or *diseño,* on the grant application. At left is such a sketch, submitted in 1839 by Domingo Sais with his (successful) application to the Mexican governor's deputy for the 6,700-acre Rancho Cañada de Herrera, now the upper Ross Valley. This sketch was made from approximately the same spot as the photograph (Bald Hill), with three-shouldered White's Hill visible at the left of both. The roughness of the sketches together with insubstantial deeds of ownership led to decades of battles in federal courts before boundaries and ownership were confirmed. Ultimately, in many cases the claimants' exploitative lawyers received the land in payment.

General Vallejo has an extensive *rancho* in this valley, upon which he has recently erected, at great expense, a very large house. Architecture, however, in this country is in its infancy. The money expended in erecting this house . . . would in the United States have raised a palace of symmetrical proportions. . . . Large herds of cattle were grazing in this valley.
—*Edwin Bryant 1846*

The Petaluma Adobe was the chief homestead of some 145,000 acres owned by General Mariano Guadalupe Vallejo between Petaluma and Fairfield, and the location of a thriving industry for the production of candles, leather goods, textiles, and metalwork. Harvests of grain, beans, peas, and lentils were gathered into its storerooms. The building, begun in 1836, was the grandest secular building of the Bay Area in Mexican times, and although its architecture failed to impress the American journalist Edwin Bryant, visiting in 1846, several features from American colonial design had been incorporated. The use of a second story, double verandah, and hipped roof were all introduced to California by American merchant Thomas Larkin in his Monterey home. Typical of Mexican buildings are the load-bearing adobe walls, found here up to four feet thick, and the absence of nails. At the left of the picture are two *hornos*, adobe ovens.

All the buildings are of adobes, or unbaked bricks, which are cemented with mud instead of mortar, and in order to protect such perishable materials from the rain, besides keeping off the rays of the sun, the houses are very neatly finished with verandas and overhanging eaves. If tolerably protected for a time, the walls, which are generally four or five feet thick, become, in a measure, vitrified, and are nearly as durable as stone. —*George Simpson 1841*

The horned cattle of California . . . are the largest and the handsomest in shape which I ever saw. There is certainly no breed in the United States equalling them in size. They, as well as the horses, subsist entirely upon the indigenous grasses, at all seasons of the year. —*Edwin Bryant 1846*

This adobe wall has stood for one and a half centuries, sheltering succeeding generations of Indians, Scots, and Americans, tenants of the land once hunted by the Olompali Coast Miwok. Adobe bricks—long used by the Spanish in Mexico and introduced by them into California—were made at the building site from clayey soil mixed with chopped straw. When dry, they weighed up to sixty pounds apiece. Seeds—such as those of the bromegrass growing at the foot of this wall—trapped in the clay give today's botanists a floral record of the times. Roof coverings were of mud, thatch, tile, or split redwood shingles. Curiously shaped stones were sought after to serve as doorsteps. About eight hundred adobe buildings were constructed in the Bay Area, of which but a few dozen remain.

Closely related to the fighting bulls of Spain, today's regal-looking Texas longhorns are descendants of Andalusian cattle brought by the Spanish to Mexico in 1521 and to San Diego in 1769. In the Bay Area, the Spanish cattle multiplied rapidly and had a marked effect on indigenous flora and fauna. Their grazing made perennial native grasses vulnerable to drought, thus giving foreign annuals the competitive edge. Overgrazing led to soil erosion and shrubs and trees were dwarfed or killed by browsing. Meanwhile bear and coyote populations flourished on carcasses left after the ranchers had removed the valued hides. So great was the litter of dry bones and skulls that fences were fashioned from them. The cows were not tame enough to milk, although one friar boasted that he was able to produce milk for a foreign guest.

An educated young gentleman was well skilled in many arts and handicrafts. He could ride . . . as well as the best cowboy of the Southwest, and with more grace; and he could throw the lasso so expertly that I have never heard of any American who was able to equal it. He could also make soap, pottery, and bricks, burn lime, tan hides, cut out and put together a pair of shoes, make candles, roll cigars, and do a great number of things that belong to different trades. —*Guadalupe de Jesús Vallejo 1840s*

The adobe building opposite, in Niles, Alameda County, was owned by José de Jesús Vallejo (General Vallejo's older brother). José's daughter Guadalupe in her later years wrote an account of the Mexican gentleman's practical skills and noted that the gentleman could also teach Indians how to do these chores; the prosperity of the ranches depended on Indian labor. Young Mexican ladies were taught to sew, embroider, and weave; writing and reading were rarely encouraged. After they married, at thirteen to fifteen years old, their duties extended to raising ten or more children, working in the kitchen, grooming menfolk's hair, making candles and soap, and sometimes sowing and harvesting. Señorita Vallejo never married, instead becoming a language teacher, skilled translator, and writer of prose and poetry.

A flower, carefully placed on head or bosom, could discreetly plead or answer a lover's suit in Mexican California, where young men and women were closely chaperoned. Of the plants pictured, yerba buena, top right, grew wild locally; below it, the Rose of Castile (*Rosa damascena*), was reportedly introduced by La Pérouse in 1786. Native to several Spanish colonies were the passionflower vine, simple dahlia near the center, and nasturtium ("red Indian cress") in the top left; below the last is a Spanish jasmine. *Hydrangea macrophylla* ("hortensia"), at the bottom, originated in the Americas and East Asia. To its left, the Monterey cypress ("evergreen") was collected from groves near Monterey and planted around cemeteries as a symbol of eternity. Ornamental plants were not commonly planted or cultivated in Mexican days, and ranch buildings were often bare of all plantings, including shade trees.

Yerba buena – I wish to be useful
White Indian cress – I wish to be a nun
Red Indian cress – my heart is dripping blood
Tuberose – I wait for thee
Red rose – thou art the queen of thy sex
White rose – thou art the queen of purity
Passion flower – hatred and rancour
Hundred leaves – I am dying for thee
Turnsol – I cannot bear the sight of thee
Dahlia – I love only thee in this world
Jasmine – thou art a coquette
Red pink – I am justified in feeling jealous
Hortensia – I want to marry thee
Violet – modesty
Geranium – I will always love thee
Evergreen – my love will be eternal
Winter gillyflower – I sigh for thee

—*José de Jesús Vallejo 1830s*

The oats' . . . usual height is about two or three feet . . . but they are frequently found even eight feet high, having a stalk half an inch in diameter. . . . [People] informed me that they had often seen many thousands of acres in a body, which were higher than they could reach when on horseback. . . . In many portions of the country, in the interior, the Indians subsist almost wholly upon them. —*Lansford Hastings 1845*

At the head of the bay it is twenty miles broad, and about the same at the southern end, where the soil is beautifully fertile, covered in summer with four or five varieties of wild clover several feet high. In many places it is overgrown with wild mustard, growing ten or twelve feet high, in almost impenetrable fields, through which roads are made like lanes. On both sides the mountains are fertile, wooded, or covered with grasses and scattered trees. —*John Charles Frémont 1846*

Many immigrants—and indeed Indians too—assumed that wild oats were indigenous to California. In fact, wild oats were introduced accidently with the missionaries' supplies and are of different species from cultivated oats. Once the wild oats took hold, they spread faster than the settlers themselves and today are the dominant grasses on many a hillside. The oat pictured here is *Avena fatua*, one of two introduced wild species. The domestic oat, sown by early missionaries, was found to yield smaller harvests than wheat or barley, so was soon abandoned as a crop.

Giant mustard plants, introduced by the Spanish, frequently sprang up from ground where cultivation had once been and since ceased. The Santa Clara Valley, as described by United States government explorer John Charles Frémont in 1846, was extraordinarily fertile, thanks to the alluvial nature of its soil and the fact that it had been so lightly cultivated. At the time of Frémont's visit, between the oak groves a few small patches of the valley floor were farmed for the subsistence of their owners, citizens of the *pueblo* of San José and the twenty or so ranchers who had title to the valley between San Francisco Bay and today's Morgan Hill. Mission Santa Clara had lost its lands, and its bells were silent, their tongues missing. The two species of mustard pictured here were photographed near Penitencia Creek, the boundary between *pueblo* land and Rancho Pala to the south.

The splendid valley, untenanted except by a few solitary *rancheros* living many miles apart, seemed to be some deserted location of ancient civilization and culture. . . . The trees have nothing of the wild growth of our forests; they are compact, picturesque, and grouped in every variety of graceful outline. The hills were covered to the summit with fields of wild oats, coloring them as far as the eye could reach, with tawny gold, against which the dark, glossy green of the oak and cypress showed with peculiar effect. — *Bayard Taylor 1850*

The parklike natural landscape that was to be seen between present-day Atherton and Los Altos on the San Francisco Peninsula was often admired by travelers who were reminded of the private estates of England, dominated by informal plantings of large deciduous trees. On this part of the Peninsula the majestic valley oak was the characteristic tree; today this landscape has all but disappeared, owing to cattle grazing, the growth of housing and industry on the floor of the Santa Clara Valley, and years of drought that have reduced many oaks to skeletons. A fragment of the lost landscape is pictured. Stanford University and a group of volunteers have undertaken to restore the once-characteristic feature of the area by replanting the university's rolling hills with young oaks.

The heavy beams that formed the mill-frame, the dam and trace, had all been constructed from the adjacent forest trees, and now that the work was completed, wanting only the saw, . . . it seemed incredible that so large a frame could be put together by so small a number of men. This saw-mill erected in the forest and of the forest, raising its long beams from the midst of the romantic scenery that surrounded it, was a glorious instance of what energy will accomplish. —*Frank Marryat 1850*

Overleaf: Seen on the previous page is a saw- and grist-mill built by Irishman John Reed on the Rancho Corte de Madera del Presidio, which he was granted in 1834. This area, in today's Marin County, had long been used as a source of redwood lumber for the San Francisco Presidio, hence the ranch's name, meaning "where wood is cut for the Presidio." In Spanish days all logging required a permit from the government. Reed's mill, erected in 1836 from weather-resistant redwood timbers secured with manzanita pegs, still stands in Mill Valley. The mill's circular saw, long vanished, was obtained from the Russians at Fort Ross in trade for elk, bear, and cattle hides.

Many foreigners foresaw that San Francisco Bay would become the watery highway of a wealthy land. Few were as authoritative as the American Alfred Robinson, who spent seventeen years in California as a trader and delivered California gold to the East Coast five years before the Gold Rush. Here the craggy East Peak of Mount Tamalpais overlooks the narrow stretch of the bay lying between the Tiburon peninsula and Richmond in the distance.

The surrounding country, diversified by hills and plains, is very beautiful; the soil is rich and heavily timbered; and the high mountains which rise around are thickly adorned with cedar-trees. There are extensive prairies also, and large tracts of excellent tillage-ground on the banks of the rivers. It is the grand region for colonization, and if peopled by our industrious backwoodsmen, who are gradually emigrating from the Western States, it must hold, in a very few years, a conspicuous station among the nations of the earth. Its locations are well adapted to purposes of agriculture, and such is its mildness of climate that all tropical fruits might be raised there, if cultivated. The large rivers are navigable for steamboats for more than one hundred miles, and are well stocked with salmon and other fish. —*Alfred Robinson 1846*

A vine with a small white flower, called here *la yerba buena*, and which, from its abundance, gives name to an island and town in the bay, was today very frequent on our road—sometimes running on the ground or climbing the trees. —*John Charles Frémont 1844*

The minty yerba buena (*Satureja douglasii*) was among the few plants that grew in the sandy northeastern part of today's San Francisco and gave its name to the area's first foreign settlement on a site south of Telegraph Hill facing onto Yerba Buena Cove. The skyscrapers of downtown San Francisco now stand in the former anchorage, and of Yerba Buena nothing remains. The "good herb" makes a refreshing tea and was used medicinally by both Indians and Spaniards. Today the plant can be found growing beneath lupine and coyotebrush on the western flank of Twin Peaks.

Descriptions of abundant wildfowl impressed prospective immigrants as an inexhaustible supply of food. The Gold Rush era proved the supply to be exhaustible. Hunting, then loss of suitable habitat to agriculture, and more recently water pollution have reduced the numbers of Bay Area waterfowl to a fifth of what they once were. Since the early decades of this century, duck hunters have been pressing government to preserve marshland against development, and now some 50,000 acres in Suisun, San Pablo, and southeast San Francisco bays are protected by state and federal governments; tens of thousands more are maintained by hunting clubs. The marshlands are home for several hundred thousand waterbirds, but in late fall migratory ducks and geese swell the numbers to millions. Here a flock of snow geese rises with a roar from feeding on a wildlife refuge in the Sacramento Valley.

D uring the winter season, California is truly a noisy, turbulent region; all the northern world seems to have given up its millions of the feathered tribes, which are here in universal convention, having complete possession of the entire country. However noisome the increasing numbers and the confused noise of these multifarious proprietors of California may be to the settlers, there is no prospect of any diminution of either, for they are assembled here by millions, merely to propagate their kind and to teach their squeaking young the art of noisy clamor. —*Lansford Hastings 1845*

Fort Ross with its gardens has a superb location. Nothing can surpass the picturesque and spectacular setting which the forests of mammoth pines that form its background supply. Ross is built in the form of a quadrilateral, 80 meters broad. In the center of this enclosure the governor's house, the officers' quarters, the arsenal, barracks, stores, and a Greek chapel surmounted by a cross and pleasant little bells, are situated. The palisade is formed by heavy timbers . . . 4 meters high, and is pierced by an opening surmounted by carronades. At opposite corners rise two hexagonal bastions two stories high, equipped with six cannon. —*Eugène Duflot de Mofras 1841*

Under authority from their government, Russians used Fort Ross and Bodega Bay in Sonoma County and the Farallon Islands as their base for sea otter hunting from 1812 to 1841. Aleut natives from Alaska were employed as hunters, and using kayaks and harpoons, they brought in 15,000 skins in the first few years. The Bodega Bay site had a good harbor but lacked lumber for the construction of an administrative center.

The architectural style of Fort Ross resembles that of Siberian blockhouses, whose builders had been recruited earlier to work in Alaska. Although Hispanic colonization was undertaken to impede Russian expansion, the Spaniards, and after them the Mexicans, poorly equipped as metalworkers, had to bring their firearms to Fort Ross for repair. In return for this and other services, the Russians were supplied with stock, seed, and foodstuffs. Eugène Duflot de Mofras, a representative of the French government, described Fort Ross in 1841 as a gladdening outpost of civilization, complete with library and classical pianist.

These settlements are made up almost entirely of foreigners; and chiefly of Americans, consisting of about two hundred persons, thirty-three of whom arrived with me in that country in the autumn of 1843, but the greater portion of them had resided there for several years previous. They all have fine herds of cattle and horses, with farms under a good state of cultivation, upon which they grow a great abundance of wheat, corn, oats, and flax, as well as a great variety and superabundance of vegetables. . . . Many of these settlers are in very prosperous circumstances, and they are all doing extremely well, considering the very short period of their residence in that country. They usually sow annually several hundred acres of wheat, from which they are not only able to supply themselves, but also to supply all the emigrants who are annually arriving, as well as to furnish much for exportation. —*Lansford Hastings 1845*

This clapboard and adobe building now stands neglected, the home of wasps, at the west end of the Sacramento Delta. It was once the home of Lansford Hastings, an American lawyer whose paean to California, *The Emigrant's Guide*, published in 1845, inspired thousands of easterners. Hastings dreamed of an American California with himself as its head of state. As part of his scheme to attract immigrants, he became the agent for a Mormon overland party that was supposed to settle around his abode in a city called Montezuma. Nothing of the city materialized, and the closest Hastings came to governorship after California's annexation was being a member of the Constitutional Convention of 1849.

On taking charge of the military post of Sonoma, I mustered my troop and found the whole force to consist of fifty men, mostly Americans, besides the usual complement of non-commissioned officers, a trumpet, a smith, and ten Indian horse boys. Our head-quarters were at the village of Sonoma, in a pleasant situation, on the line of communication with San Francisco and the Sacramento valley, being central as between those points and Bodega and Ross, on the coast. Our barracks were roomy and commodious, and we had an abundant supply of horses. —*Joseph Warren Revere 1846*

On July 9, 1846, U.S. Navy Lieutenant Joseph Revere raised the Stars and Stripes in Sonoma, replacing the Bear Flag, emblem of a band of independence-minded Americans who had rebelled against Mexico a month earlier. The lieutenant's barracks, seen above, were formerly occupied by Mexican Army troops under General Vallejo and were built during the 1830s. Today, the state parks department has again raised a Mexican flag, which flies from the balcony. Sonoma rivaled the town of Yerba Buena in importance until the Gold Rush. Now it is the only town in the Bay Area that retains something of the feel of a Mexican *pueblo* with its central plaza and low adobe houses.

Heavy to Get,
Light to Hold

Gold Rush San Francisco

Gold rush poster printed in Boston

W hat would have happened if the Gold Rush had enriched Mexico rather than the United States? Perhaps the Bay Area's valleys and hills would still be Mexican, barely recognizable under the mantle of a more agricultural society.

As it was, a millworker on the American River brought up a nugget of gold in January of 1848—a month before the Treaty of Guadalupe-Hidalgo and formal annexation of California by the United States—and the news sailed across the world. San Francisco became an instant ghost town when its nine hundred or so inhabitants fled for the gold country. Farmhands, sailors, and soldiers dropped their hoes, ropes, and muskets and followed. News of the find soon reached Mexico, the Sandwich Islands, and South America, and by the end of the year over six thousand impetuous young men had passed through San Francisco. By early 1849 shiploads of Yankees and Chinese were arriving, and the harbor turned into a bare forest of ships' masts, the vessels abandoned. Thousands of others trudged overland from Missouri, five months away. During the Sierra's stormy winter season, San Francisco, the miners' depot, swelled into a tent and shack city of men waiting to cross over the bay or travel up the Sacramento River to the mines.

The more canny newcomers realized that miners were a more reliable source of wealth than mines and set up shop as merchants, landlords, and gambling-hall owners. Ships' hulls were used as storehouses, hotels, and jails. By 1849 entrepreneurs were importing thousands of prefabricated houses to fill the need left by carpenters-turned-miners, and San Francisco began to take on the appearance of a permanent city. Portsmouth Plaza, the social center of the frontier city, lay one block from the beach,

Ship's compass

but in no time wooden wharves extended the streets into deeper water. The city auctioned off subdivided mudflats in the cove's shallows, thus encouraging the new owners to fill the "water lots" with refuse and the spoils from leveled sandhills; soon Portsmouth Plaza was left far from the shore. Today, the plaza is a park in the heart of Chinatown.

Eastward across the bay was a fertile plain of live oaks backed by redwood forests. The future site of Oakland had every advantage over San Francisco—except the sheltered deep-water harbor that was the crucial factor in San Francisco's ascendancy. The first Americans to settle in the East Bay logged the hills, ignoring the Peralta family's title to the land, and shipped the lumber from the San Antonio Estuary. Oakland was founded by squatters in 1852, and by the time the last redwood was felled in about 1860, the town's residents had turned to agriculture and commerce. A regular ferry service carried the first commuters to San Francisco.

301 Pennsylvania Avenue, San Francisco

Early San Francisco was a rough place. A lawless town frequently leveled by fires, in winter its unpaved streets became quagmires. However shifting and dissolute the city, it was the new frontier and a vulnerable one of strategic importance. The federal government ordered the construction of solid forts and batteries around the harbor's mouth for its defense, and an arsenal at Benicia on Carquinez Strait.

Benicia Arsenal, Solano County

Off the beaten track between San Francisco and the mines, the land lay undisturbed and uncultivated, but the air rang with the blasts of hunters shooting every edible creature that flew or crawled. The region's cattle had already been consumed by miners. One-third of a million seabirds' eggs were pillaged yearly from the Farallon Islands. With the near extermination of wildlife, thousand-mile cattle drives moved toward San Francisco's cookhouses, and other provender was shipped in from Hawaii, Australia, and Chile.

By 1854 San Francisco's population had reached about forty thousand (twenty times that of the adobe village of Los Angeles). The season of the freelance miner was drawing to a close, and the city's banks were becoming the key to mining operations. Five hundred tons of gold—an amount that would fill a small living room—had already been brought to San Francisco. Only corporations could provide the capital demanded by hard-rock and hydraulic California gold mining and later by Nevada silver mining. San Francisco tours of those days took visitors to dozens of buildings deriving their wealth from the large-scale mines, and the state commissioned surveyors to locate more sources of the precious minerals.

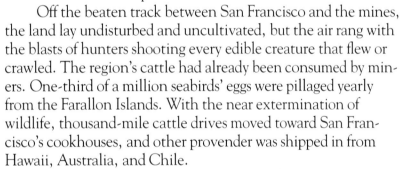

Benjamin G. Lathrop House, Redwood City, San Mateo County

Seal of the City of San Francisco, 1852–1859

The Gold Rush city has almost entirely vanished, and the gold itself is scattered throughout the world, unrecognized. Yet how tenacious is that era's grip on our imagination! ❧

G old, gold, gold, gold!
 Bright and yellow, hard and cold,
 Molten, graven, hammered, rolled,
Heavy to get and light to hold;
Hoarded, bartered, bought, and sold,
Stolen, bartered, squandered, doled,
Spurned by the young but hugged by the old
To the very verge of the churchyard mould;
Price of many a crime untold.
Gold, gold, gold, gold!
Good or bad a thousandfold.

—*Anonymous*

This four-inch-high gold-encrusted rock was brought up from a mine in Placer County. The most direct method of California gold extraction was to locate the gold-bearing seam and then forcefully separate the metal from the rock; only this method could produce such a sample. Placer miners let the frosts and storms of millennia do much of the work for them and then sluiced the creekbeds where the gold had become concentrated. Hydraulic miners used powerful waterhoses to wash out the gold concentrated in ancient, disused creekbeds, and then sluiced. All of the hard-won gold passed through San Francisco, transforming the village into a city.

All hands have left me but two; they will stay till the cargo is landed and ballast in, then they will go. Both mates will leave in a few days, and then I will have only the two boys, and I am fearful that they will run. . . . There's no help to be got at any price. The store ship that sailed from here ten days ago took three of my men at $100 per month; there is nothing that anchors but what loses their men. —*Christopher Allyn 1848*

At some future period, when the site of San Francisco may be explored by a generation ignorant of its history, it will take its place by the side of Herculaneum and Pompeii, and furnish many valuable relics to perplex the prying Antiquarian. Buried in the streets, from six to ten feet beneath the surface, there is already a stratum of artificial productions which the entombed cities of Italy cannot exhibit. Knives, forks, spoons, chisels, files, and hardware of every description, gathered from the places of several conflagrations. Masses of nails exhibiting volcanic indications, stove-plates and tin-ware, empty bottles by the cart-load and hundreds of other miscellanies, lie quietly and deeply interred in Sacramento street, and perhaps will be carefully exhumed in days to come, and distributed over the world as precious relics. —*Evening Picayune 1850*

Scores of ships from the East Coast were abandoned at the end of their half-year voyages around the Horn, and some of the hulls were absorbed into San Francisco when the muddy shallows were filled and wharves became streets. Many years later these hulls have come to light during excavations in the financial district, formerly Yerba Buena Cove. Salvaged from a construction site was the ship's knee pictured at the left. Made from the trunk and root of a tree, it stands about five feet high and joined the ship's deck to the hull.

Every article in this photograph was "carefully exhumed" (as anticipated by a *Picayune* satirist in 1850) from a site north of Telegraph Hill in 1978, then marked with a seven-digit museum reference number. The "precious relics" include mineral water bottles from the 1860s, dumped behind a seawall.

Construction of houses has for a long time been the best speculative investment you could make. Therefore, building styles have come from all parts of the world, prepared in advance. . . . Each nation has supplied its own [style]. England has flooded the place with houses of sheet iron, tin, cast iron, zinc, or laminated iron; these types are not much liked, and if the shippers get back their expenses, they will have to consider themselves lucky. Small wooden houses have come in great numbers from Sweden, France, and other countries, but especially from America. China has sent an enormous contingent. —*Etienne Derbec 1850*

Several thousand disassembled houses were shipped to San Francisco during the Gold Rush years—some were even packed across the Isth-

This house, built on the side of Telegraph Hill, is a survivor from 1852, when San Francisco's population stood at about thirty-six thou-

mus of Panama—and redistributed among the new towns on the shores of the bay. Forests were plentiful locally, but willing sawyers and carpenters were not. Virtually all of San Francisco's Gold Rush era housing was destroyed in the frequent fires the city suffered in its first decade or in the earthquake and fire of 1906. Imported houses survive in other parts of the Bay Area: pictured above, left, is the Vásquez House, almost certainly prefabricated in Sweden with forty others, imported by the Scandinavian consul, and erected in Sonoma.

This town has been twice laid in ashes, but the young Phoenix has risen on ampler wings than those which steadied the consumed form of its parent. Even with its heart burnt out, it looks like the skeleton of a great city. That heart will be reconstructed and send the lifeblood leaping through the arteries. —*Walter Colton 1849*

sand. The most common architectural style was a simplified Greek Revival from New England, the houses painted white with green shutters. Many of the city's fires were intentionally set, either to destroy a competitor's merchandise or to give vent to a grudge. The citizens' energy for reconstruction earned the phoenix—a mythical bird whose deathbed and cradle are fire— a place on the city's seal.

The various wharves continued to stretch eastward, as if it were intended that they should soon connect Yerba Buena Island with the mainland. The sand hills behind supplied ample materials for filling up the bay, and . . . no sooner was a water lot piled and capped than up sprang a frame building upon it; no sooner was the hollow beneath filled than the house of wood was destroyed, and replaced by some elegant brick or granite structure. —*Frank Soulé 1852*

It has grown out of the mud a beauty. It is the handsomest building in this town, and it is admirably built from the driving of the piles to the minutest parts. . . . I enjoy it as much as an artist does a fine picture. —*William Tecumseh Sherman 1854*

The original line of Yerba Buena Cove's beach is marked by present-day Montgomery Street. The Belli Building (as it is now called) was built on wooden planks laid on the soft ground in about 1851, as a tobacco warehouse; to the left of it is the Genella Building, built as a chinaware store. By 1854 the shoreline had moved six blocks to the east and was finally fixed by a seawall construction project that continued from 1877 to 1914. The first buildings erected in the cove were of wood, and stood on pilings over the water; subsequently, fill was taken from nearby rocky hills and sand dunes and thrown into the cove to form the foundation for newer masonry buildings. An eighty-foot-high sand dune long stood near Market and Second streets, and another prominent landmark, Rincon Hill, occupied the area between Spear, Second, Folsom, and Brannan streets. Rincon Hill was destroyed by street gradings, and doubtless much of it went into Mission Bay, filled in the 1870s. Sandfill was of questionable solidity: in the winter of 1852, parts of Jackson Street sank four to five feet, and one theater settled several inches on opening night.

The bank building of Lucas, Turner, and Co. was erected in 1854 at Montgomery and Gold streets to serve miners and merchants, with William Tecumseh Sherman (later of Civil War fame) as its manager. Rising from ninety-six piles, it was constructed with bricks from China, pillars of ships' masts, and finely cut granite facing for the ground floor. Originally the building consisted of three stories with tall pedimented windows, but the upper stories were partially destroyed in the earthquake and fire of 1906.

F ort Point is to be built with the aim of] securing this important harbor, the key to our immensely valuable possessions on the Pacific; the depot of a commerce equalled by [only] a few of the Atlantic cities, the harbor of refuge in time of war of our whaling fleets, and of our whole commercial marine on the Pacific, a depot of supply of all our military forces on this ocean and this coast. —*J. G. Barnard c. 1853*

San Francisco's Fort Point was part of a new defense system planned to include a fort on Alcatraz Island and batteries on Lime Point, Angel Island, and at today's Fort Mason. The range of the guns of the time dictated strategic positions for the fortifications. Pictured is a smoothbore Rodman gun that had a range of two miles. The fine architecture of Fort Point was influenced by the ideas of Brigadier General Simon Bernard, formerly a military engineer for Napoleon, and displays a complex vaulting pattern of brick, with precise granite detailing. Some of the materials for the construction, at an early stage supervised by Major J. G. Barnard, were taken from the earlier Mexican battery built higher up on the same bluff; granite came from China as ship's ballast, and from Folsom, near Sacramento. By 1862 when the fort was completed, new rifled artillery with a ten-mile range rendered such masonry

forts obsolete and called for concealed guns outside the Golden Gate. The structure was never put to the test, and Fort Point survives intact today, situated under an arch of the Golden Gate Bridge and incorporated into the Golden Gate National Recreation Area.

This is one of the finest public buildings in the state, and as it stands in a commanding position, presents a most imposing appearance from the bays and Straits of Carquinez. . . . The hall is connected with the steamboat landing by a fine new plank sidewalk leading through the main street of the town, and by all the principal hotels, Post Office and stores. —*Placer Times and Transcript 1852*

Benicia's City Hall was newly built in 1852, designed by Lloyd Rider in the formal early Greek Revival style rare in California. The town, named after General Mariano Guadalupe Vallejo's wife, was the bright star in the hopes of several wealthy investors, situated as it was on the water route into the interior and having deep-water access. In 1853–54, the building enjoyed brief glory as the State Capitol for the bilingual legislature. That era has recently been recreated with period furnishings installed by the California Department of Parks and Recreation, which maintains the building as a state historic park.

Raphael Garcier . . . does grant and demise unto [James A. Shorb and William J. Mercer] . . . the privilege of building lime kilns—quarrying and using limestone wood for burning the kilns and entire timber privilege of the Rancho for the space of ten years. . . . [The grantees shall pay to Garcier] one third of all the lime burnt . . . and for all the redwood spruce or pine timber . . . four dollars per tree. . . . [They] are not to cut any trees measuring over three feet across the butt. . . . [Garcier agrees] to furnish oxens carts and Indians to haul all the lime burnt in the kiln or kilns to the embarcadero, and assist in loading or putting the lime in the vessels. . . . [The grantees] shall have the privilege of cultivating ten acres of land for gardening or other purposes and the privilege of grazing such stock as they may need in conducting or carrying on their operations. —*Legal contract 1850*

The origin of the three kilns built in the rift valley of the San Andreas fault near Olema in Marin County was long a mystery. Large Douglas-firs growing from the ruins apparently predated American occupation, yet Russians and Spaniards would have had little or no use for lime, used in cement and whitewash. A legal contract concerning the kilns was brought to light in the 1940s and ended the controversy by dating them to 1850, when lime was in demand for fireproof brick buildings in San Francisco. Production at these kilns must have stopped suddenly, for the kiln on the right of the photograph is still loaded with limestone ready for firing.

John Marsh, Esq., of Contra Costa County . . . has now nearly completed probably the most beautiful and complete private residence in the State of California. . . . [It] is situated in the centre of the plain. . . . From a quarry which has been opened upon the estate, an abundant supply of stone for the building has been obtained. It is of the finest quality of freestone, of a beautiful drab or cream color, slightly variegated. . . . The architect, Thomas Boyd, Esq., . . . with a true artistic perception of what was wanted in the building to make it harmonize with the surrounding scenery, has departed from the stereotyped square box . . . called a home in California, and has adopted the old English domestic style of architecture—a pleasing and appropriate union of Manor House and Castle. —*Daily Evening Bulletin 1856*

In early American California, stone residences were admired as a sign of permanence in a transient society and were (and still are) uncommon. This imposing mansion was built for Dr. John Marsh on his seventeen-thousand-acre ranch east of Mount Diablo in 1856. The outlying location of the ranch, settled by Marsh in 1837, had made it the first outpost of civilization for many an early immigrant over the Sierra. Replacing an adobe, the new house was to be Marsh's bridal home, but he was murdered by his own disgruntled cattlemen two weeks after its completion. Its original stone tower was toppled in 1868 by an earthquake along the Hayward fault, and was replaced by the wooden one seen in the photograph. The house is currently being restored by the state.

There was little reason to wait for domestic animals to fatten when the land, air, and water were teeming with wildlife. The native or Olympia

oyster (above) was abundant in San Francisco Bay and tasty but relatively small. Indians left behind vast mounds of shells at the bay's edge, and dredged shells for many years supplied the cement industry in San Mateo County and chicken feed manufacturers in Sonoma County. From the 1870s eastern, and later Japanese, oysters were farmed in San Francisco Bay and reached a production of over seven thousand tons a year. By 1910, the industry went into a decline because of water pollution. Japanese ("Pacific") oysters are cultivated today in the clean coastal bays of Marin County.

The San Francisco bills of fare present at all seasons great variety, and no one has a right to complain who has but to choose from bear, elk, deer, antelope, turtle, hares, partridges, quails, wild geese, brant, numerous kinds of ducks, snipe, plover, curlew, cranes, salmon, trout, and other fish, and *oysters*.

It is not until you have been a long time without an oyster that you find how indispensable to your complete happiness this bivalve is. —*Frank Marryat 1851*

The tiger cat is a beautiful animal, and very ferocious for its size: we saw two or three of these, about the size of a wild cat, and beautifully marked in the coat. I shot but one, and it was with the greatest difficulty that I could induce him to resign his life without having his skin spoilt.
—*Frank Marryat 1850*

Off the beaten track to the mines, the animal realm lay undisturbed—for the moment. For naturalists such as John Woodhouse Audubon,

Naturalists and curious travelers of the mid-nineteenth century used the gun in place of the camera. Handsome bobcats drew the attention of the English gentleman Frank Marryat, who was camping in northern Sonoma County to escape the clamor of civilization, and he left us an engaging record of his stay. A *rancho* and later a town—Los Gatos, in Santa Clara County—were named after the bobcat, and the animal, unique to North America, is still found in many parts of the Bay Area and hunted in several of California's wilder counties.

There is no trail but that of the horses and elk, all terminating at some waterhole, not a sign of civilization, not the track of a white man to be seen, and sometimes the loneliness and solitude seem unending. —*John W. Audubon 1849*

the thirty-seven-year-old son of the more famous John James Audubon, this was a precious opportunity. The younger man arrived in the northern San Joaquin Valley with a dozen companions in late 1849 after a nine-month overland journey from New York and made sketches of mammals and birds for his father. Unfortunately his work was lost with the steamer *Central America*. Pictured are the hoofprints of a tule elk, one of Point Reyes National Seashore's protected herd.

There is no delight of the senses quite equal to that of inhaling the fragrance of the wild California herb. . . . It is a whitish, woolly plant, resembling life everlasting, and exudes, when mature, a thick aromatic gum. For leagues on leagues the air is flavored with it—a rich, powerful, balsamic smell, almost a *taste*, which seems to dilate the lungs like mild ether. To inhale such an air is perfect ecstasy. It does not cloy, like other odors; but strengthens with a richer tonic than the breath of budding pines. . . . It stirs the blood like a trumpet, and makes the loftiest inspiration easy. I write poems, I paint pictures, I carve statues, I create history. If I should live to be old, and feel my faculties failing, I shall go back to restore the sensations of youth in that wonderful air. —*Bayard Taylor 1859*

The pungent aroma of sagebrush (*Artemisia californica*) is enhanced by the moist air of the shrub's favored habitat, the coastal slopes, and for many Californians is the smell of home. The journalist Bayard Taylor, eloquent chronicler of the Gold Rush era, avowedly fell under its charm. Alongside Highway 1 it rattles in the wind against coyotebrush and lupine, while inland in the Diablo Range, it mingles with chamise and manzanita and becomes partly deciduous to survive summer's heat and drought.

Early morning winter fog, opposite, seen from the peak of Mount Diablo, is drawn toward the coast (to the right in the photograph). The wide fog-blanketed valley in the distance is San Ramon, and in the far distance rise the Santa Cruz Mountains. Since 1851 Mount Diablo (elevation 3849 feet) has been the major reference point for surveys in northern California and was often in the sights of surveying instruments used by William Brewer, commissioned by the state government to map the land and prospect for minerals.

Friday found us astir early, and we came on. The valleys and canyons and the distant bay were all covered with dense fog, but we were above it, looking down on its top. As the sun came up this fog seemed a sea of the purest white, the mountains rising through it as islands and the tall trees often rising above its surface. It was now tossed into huge billows by the morning breeze, and as the sun rose higher it curled up. The scenes gradually shifted as the curtain rolled away, and the mountain landscape was itself again. —*William Brewer 1861*

revious to 1848 the river [Sacramento] was noted for the
purity of its waters, flowing from the mountains as clear as
crystal; but since the discovery of gold, the "washings" render it as muddy and turbid as is the Ohio at spring flood . . . dis-
coloring even the waters of the great Bay into which it empties.
— *William Brewer 1862*

It was five o'clock before we left and after sundown before we got on our mules, with at least fifteen miles to ride. Night closed on us among a labyrinth of hills and canyons twelve miles from camp and at least six from any road. We gave our mules the bridle and let them find the way back, which they did with a sagacity beyond belief, over steep hills, along ridges, through canyons, to the road at the foot of the hills at the edge of the plain. — *William Brewer 1861*

Placer mining began the silting up of the rivers that feed San Francisco Bay, but the chief cause of river and bay siltation was soon hydraulic mining, which washed away mountainsides to free the gold. A volume of rock and soil equivalent to a third of San Bruno Mountain was set in motion on a two-hundred-mile journey toward the Golden Gate, causing shoaling of navigation channels, flooding, and destruction of marine life. Worked from 1853 to 1884, the Malakoff Diggins in Nevada County (opposite) were the site of the second-largest hydraulic mining operation in the Sierra Nevada. In 1884 hydraulic mining was effectively banned, but the Sacramento River (lower photo) and San Francisco Bay continued to receive silt from it up to the middle of this century. Today much siltation is caused by agriculture, which exposes the soil to the erosive forces of irrigation, wind, and weather.

The dry hills of the Diablo Range (upper photo), seen here from Mission Peak, were traveled on mule-back by the indefatigable surveyor William Brewer on his way to the Santa Clara Valley. By his own reckoning, during his four years in California, Brewer traveled "horseback (or mule) 6,560 miles; on foot 2,772; public conveyance 4,175—total of 13,507 miles, or enough to reach halfway around the earth." The diary of his travels, *Up and Down California in 1860– 1864,* is a priceless account of the day-to-day pleasures and labors entailed in adding California's rugged topography into the scientific record.

Come One!
Come All!

Come one! Come all!
Our state is wide and long, and your welcome, to the best we have, is hearty.

Socialite and amateur firefighter Lillie Coit returning from a night on the town

Quicksilver mine, New Almaden, Santa Clara County

Speculation in merchandise and building lots—the driving force of early San Francisco—thrived on increasing demand. So when the rush for gold was over, San Francisco promoted the state's other riches: books, broadsheets, and newspapers all proclaimed California a cornucopia of agricultural wealth and opportunity. Until the 1890s, the Bay Area rode proudly on this tide of profitable publicity.

Land was cleared of brush and trees for pasture. Farmers fenced out cattle and produced giant vegetables and towering crops from the virgin soils of the valleys and newly diked delta of the Sacramento and San Joaquin rivers. From the earth's bowels were mined quicksilver, coal, and oil. Salt was raked from evaporation ponds along the bay's edge. Redwood, the builder's dream lumber, fell to the logger's axe, and tanbark oaks of the San Francisco Peninsula were barked for the cattle hide tanneries. This was a time of reckless optimism and confidence in human omnipotence. "Every valley shall be exalted and every mountain and hill made low; the crooked shall be made straight, and the rough places plain," prophesied Isaiah (40:4), and Californians had taken it upon themselves to fulfill the prophesy.

Towns were founded even before title to the land was confirmed, and streets were laid out in little more time than it took to draw a grid pattern on paper. Some towns had a good economic reason for existing; others with names such as New York of the Pacific or New Chicago depended on a group act of faith fostered by a developer. Those towns that became realities were architectural echoes of eastern cities stirred into a cacophony of styles and imitations of styles all dubbed Victorian. Only the effusiveness of decoration and the universality of the bay window

Black Diamond Mines Regional Park, Contra Costa County

Site proposed for New Chicago, Santa Clara County

were distinctive of local architecture. Gardens too were crowded with old favorites, often brought out west by brides leaving their childhood homes.

The completion of the transcontinental railroad in 1869, bringing New York just eight days away, ended the Bay Area's isolation. Everything from disassembled steamships to live baby oysters arrived by rail and was unloaded on Oakland's two-mile-long wharf jutting out toward Yerba Buena Island. Fabulous fruits and vegetables and eggs went eastward over the Sierra's summit.

San Francisco became the Queen of the West, and by the century's end Oakland had grown from a quiet suburb into a city. From the 1870s San Francisco's more leisured citizens were seeking secluded country estates within reach of railroads in the sylvan surroundings of Atherton and Menlo Park, and later Burlingame. These estates were to become suburban conglomerations in the next century. When in 1875 the Northern Pacific Coast Railroad linked Sausalito with points north to Tomales, San Francisco office workers found they could commute by train and ferry from relatively bucolic Marin. The Bay Area had become a place of which the famed conservationist John Muir, a sometime resident of the East Bay, could write, "I was terribly dazed and confused with the dust and din and heavy sticky air of that low region." His respite was found only in the Sierra Nevada; less phobic citizens visited resorts or took a ride in Golden Gate Park.

In this ebullient period the groundwork was laid for land use patterns that are still evident in town plans, ports, and agricultural enclaves, all under stress brought on by a vastly increased population. Much nineteenth-century architecture has survived termite, fire, and bulldozer. Some is disguised in the name of modernization, some neglected but serviceable, some lovingly restored. All are precious landmarks in a changing world. ❧

Haas-Lilienthal House, San Francisco

Winchester Mystery House, San Jose

Conservatory of Flowers, Golden Gate Park, San Francisco

Nobody seems to think of building a sober house. . . .
Of all the efflorescent, floriated bulbousness, and flamboyant craziness that ever decorated a city, I think San Francisco may carry off the prize. And yet, such is the glittering and metallic brightness of the air, when it is not surcharged with fog, that I am not sure but this riotous run of architectural fancy is just what the city needs to redeem its otherwise hard nakedness.
—*Noah Brooks 1883*

San Francisco's late Victorian architecture was as exuberant as it was scorned by critics. Some styles were gaudily painted displays of virtuoso woodwork; others seemed respectable stonework in sober colors but rang hollow to the touch. Ninety percent of nineteenth-century San Francisco was built of redwood. The pedigree of the Queen Anne style (pictured), a new fashion in 1883, has been traced back to an English architect working in decorative brick; thence down to an incarnation in wood created in Rhode Island; and so to California, where "Queen Anne" was a catchall name for any large house with a prominent gable and curved forms. Of forty-eight thousand Victorian houses built in San Francisco between 1850 and 1915, one-third have survived and give much of the city its distinctive character.

Early morning fog envelops Mount Olympus, opposite, one of San Francisco's forty-two hills. The sand that so plagued the early city was blown eastward from what is now the Sunset district, through gaps in the rocky hills, to form dunes where it settled. Mount Olympus and neighboring Mount Sutro and Twin Peaks are largely composed of reddish chert and greenstone of the Franciscan formation.

It is a city where houses seem to have literally been built
Upon sand.
A city climbing up the sides of sandhills,
Overlooked and girt and crowned by sandhills;
A city the color of dust and ashes;
A summerless, winterless city,
Where men and women have no season of change
In the substance of garments;
Where you may wear furs if you like them in July or December.

Convert the hills of Rome into dust heaps
And plant them around the harbor of Queenstown;
Crowd on their sides a city made up indiscriminately of
The Strand, Broadway, Wapping, Donnybrook,
Hongkong, Denver, Vera Cruz, and Hamburg
And you may create in your mind's eye
Something like an adequate picture of San Francisco.

—*Justin McCarthy 1871*

The . . . hotel, like most American buildings, is constructed on the pattern of a ship. It is a large wooden box whose single roof covers entire floors of rooms heaped one above the other, all joined by mahogany staircases with metal-edged steps. The rooms have windows to the street or to various light-wells. What we call a *patio* is unknown in this country, and its absence drives people into the street as if fearful of asphyxiation. —*Guillermo Prieto 1877*

Mexican Californians witnessed the total eclipse of Hispanic architecture, and judging by the readiness of many of them to conceal adobe walls behind wood siding, install large windows, or replace their old houses altogether, they were hardly sorry to see it go. Guillermo Prieto, a Mexican exile in the Bay Area, described the striking contrast between the old style and the new, born of different climates and material resources, and evidently preferred the old and familiar. Pictured above is the old Burlington Hotel of Port Costa, new when Prieto visited the Bay Area in 1877.

Frame houses and even churches were moved for many reasons: to match the new ground level when streets were graded; to vacate a valuable site; and in at least one case, after a divorce half the house was moved across town. The house shown here was moved recently when land was divided among family members. Others have been moved to create historic districts in San Francisco, Oakland, and San Jose.

If the site should fail to please the owner, he buys another, has his house with everything therein, raised and placed on wheels; and a two-story house is seen slowly wending its way through the streets, while inside, perhaps, the housewife is cooking the midday meal for her family. Where you are, such a thing would attract attention; but here all one hears at the most is the scolding of a few draymen with lighter vehicles, who have to turn around because the big vehicle blocks the whole street, and who make a detour to reach their destination. —*Eugene Bandel 1859*

Kearny, Montgomery, Market, California and Sacramento streets are characteristic in their magnificence and wealth. The first of these is about two miles long. The lowest level of its buildings is made up of broad panes of glass held between slender iron columns, giving the effect of open space, so that the mass of the structures above seems to rest on air. With unvarying uniformity the walls are broken by rows of windows, all the same size, all with green blinds. Only here and there the monotony is interrupted by elegant porticos, urns, fountains, and statues, which except for their unsubstantial materials would be miracles of architectural achievement. —*Guillermo Prieto 1877*

On either side of an alleyway, the two elegant Italianate buildings of Anson P. Hotaling's liquor business on Jackson Street were typical of downtown San Francisco of the 1860s and 1870s. Following the city fires of the early 1850s, wood construction was banned from the central district, and these brick buildings were fitted with iron shutters as an added precaution. Happily they survived the earthquake and fire of 1906, and Hotaling's liquor business continued until Prohibition.

San Francisco July 14th 1861 —

This Octigon House was built and owned by Wm C. McElroy and his wife Harriet S. McElroy and is intended as our privet Residence, we have only one daughter aged nine Years, my wife is a native of Lancaster Pa. and her maiden name was "Shober" (aged 40 Years) I am a native of Virginia "aged 42 Years) and we are a very good Looking old Couple and pretty we off in this world, goods. My wife landed in this City in 1849 and I arrive here in 1851 and of Course as, you will perceive we was married in the City of ... school name Emma Eliza ... serve to ... picture herewith ... the ... A. Wolfe an ... that he ... spectacle business by the time that ... ony to ... obli... them ...

But is the square form the best of all? Is the right angle the best angle? Can not some radical improvement be made, both in the outside form and the internal arrangement of our houses? Nature's forms are mostly spherical. She makes ten thousand curvilineal to one square figure. Then why not apply her forms to houses? Fruits, eggs, tubers, nuts, grains, seeds, trees, etc., are made spherical, in order to inclose the most material in the least compass. Since . . . a circle includes more space for its surface, than any other form, of course the nearer spherical our houses, the more inside room for the outside wall, besides being more comfortable. —*Orson Fowler 1848*

A Home for All, a manifesto written by the phrenologist and amateur architect Orson Fowler, advanced the theory that the form of one's home

governed mental and physical health. The circle was the ideal shape, but he conceded that the octagon was the closest practical one. Fowler's followers built a rash of octagonal houses across the country, including at least five in San Francisco. Pictured opposite is Octagon House on Gough Street, built in 1861 by William McElroy and his wife, who embedded in the structure a time capsule containing the letter reproduced in the photograph. The staircase shown above ascends into the cupola. Octagon House is now maintained as a museum by the National Society of Colonial Dames in California.

Quarrying and street grading to accommodate San Francisco's grid pattern of streets have left scars on many of the city's hills. Rincon Hill in the South of Market district, and Irish Hill, once near Third and Twentieth streets, were nearly leveled. The east side of Telegraph Hill (pictured) was quarried for its ballast and fill materials for decades. And from 1892 to 1912, Gray Brothers quarried relentlessly, bringing inhabited hilltop houses crashing to the bottom. After repeated outcries against the activity, one year the brothers resorted to using the cover of Fourth of July festivities to detonate their own charges and bring more of the hill tumbling down.

A two story frame dwelling of a dozen rooms, furnished, unoccupied, crashed over the southeast brink of Telegraph Hill, near Green and Sansome Sts., about nine o'clock yesterday morning, and was reduced to kindling wood nearly 200 ft. below. A portion of the house adjoining was left suspended over the precipice, and is in imminent danger of following its neighbor to destruction.

Continuous blasting by Gray Brothers and loosening of earth by the recent rains are responsible for this climax of a series of disturbances that has kept the hilltop community in a state of terror for years past. —*San Francisco Chronicle 1907*

Nearly all the fine opportunities that the hill contours offered, to compensate by dignity of aspect for the dreariness of the summers, have been wasted. . . . These hills have been outraged and insulted with manifold cruelties: never finished grading undertakings have uselessly torn them in some places; . . . the perfectly straight streets disfigure, as with long cruel stripes, the sturdy forms of the noble hills. For these streets pass over the hills in mercilessly undeviating parallel lines.
—*Josiah Royce 1886*

In 1839 Francisco de Haro, the first *alcalde* (mayor) of San Francisco, commissioned the Swiss Jean Jacques Vioget to project a plan for the growth of the fledgling town. For the following sixty years the alignment of the road to the mission and those first few blocks at Yerba Buena Cove dictated the street pattern of what became a city encompassing almost unassailable hills and hemmed by a very unconforming coastline. Adherence to the grid makes surveying easy and travel today simple and dramatic, but discourages the formation of neighborhoods and ignores the fine views the terrain could offer householders. Among the grid pattern's notable detractors have been Gold Rush journalist Bayard Taylor; Josiah Royce, philosopher and historian; and California's chronicler, Hubert H. Bancroft. Shown here are Eureka and Noe valleys as seen from Corona Heights.

Neither in beauty of greensward, nor in great umbrageous trees, do these special conditions of the topography, soil, and climate of San Francisco allow us to hope that any pleasure ground it can acquire will ever compare in the most distant degree with those of New York or London.

There is not a full-grown tree of beautiful proportions near San Francisco, nor have I seen any young trees that promised fairly, except perhaps, of certain compact, clumpy forms of evergreens, wholly wanting in grace and cheerfulness. It would not be wise nor safe to undertake to form a park upon any plan which assumed as a certainty that trees which would delight the eye can be made to grow near San Francisco. —*Frederick Law Olmsted 1865*

Frederick Law Olmsted, creator of New York's Central Park, believed that San Francisco's terrain and climate would never support a resplendent park. He proposed a sunken, linear park meandering in a southwest-northeast direction west of Van Ness Avenue. Cheaper land was available farther west, however, and in 1871 the city employed William Hammond Hall to begin the conversion of a thousand acres of poor soil and shifting sands into a new park. Hall's work was largely confined to the eastern section, where native live oaks had already established a footing. The major challenge was subsequently taken up by John McLaren, who reclaimed the sand dunes by planting marram grass, followed by shrubs and trees nourished on "street sweepings" (horse manure). Paddocks were built for elk, bison, and other animals—the very animals being hunted to near-extinction in the wild. After fifty-six years as park superintendent, McLaren died in 1943, leaving plans for still more extensive plantings. The Conservatory, pictured below, copied from one in Kew Gardens, London, was erected in 1883.

The cable cars have for all practical purposes made San Francisco a dead level. They take no count of rise or fall, but slide equably on their appointed courses from one end to the other of a six-mile street. They turn corners almost at right angles, cross other lines, and for aught I know may run up the sides of houses. There is no visible agency of their flight, but once in a while you shall pass a five-storied building humming with machinery that winds up an everlasting wire cable, and the initiated will tell you that here is the mechanism. I gave up asking questions. If it pleases Providence to make a car run up and down a slit in the ground for many miles, and if for twopence halfpenny I can ride in that car, why shall I seek the reasons of the miracle?—*Rudyard Kipling 1879*

The inventor of San Francisco's cable car system, Andrew S. Hallidie, took the technology of shaft mines and used it to scale the city's precipitous hills. He had the encouragement of the Society for the Prevention of Cruelty to Animals, which was anxious to see horses pulling omnibuses and streetcars spared debilitating and dangerous hill work.

Nob and Russian hills were made accessible and became valuable sites for residences of the wealthy. Without the invention of the cable car, the hills might well have been lowered. The first trial run was on Clay Street between Kearny and Jones streets in 1873. With instant popularity, cable cars proliferated, reaching a zenith in the 1890s: San Francisco had over twenty-five miles of line, and cable cars ran in Oakland, Chicago, New York City, and even in New Zealand. Pictured are cars built for the Sutter Street Railway Company in 1878. Twice in the past fifty years San Francisco's cable car system has been saved from oblivion. Today the "building humming with machinery," as the English author Rudyard Kipling described it, is at Washington and Mason streets, its cables drawing cars crammed with sightseers over five miles of line.

This burial place . . . adjoins that devoted to the city paupers, out among the melancholy sand dunes by the ocean shore. It is parcelled off by white fences into inclosures for a large number of separate burial guilds, or *tongs*. . . . It is the practice of these people to convey the bones of their dead to China, but preliminary funerals take place in regular form. . . . The bones are left in the ground a year or more before being in a fit condition for removal, and over these the rites of propitiation are performed. . . . The provisions were unloaded, and taken up and laid on small wooden altars, of which there is one in the front of each plot. Most conspicuous among them were numerous whole roast pigs decorated with ribbons and colored papers. There were besides, roast fowls, rice, salads, sweetmeats, fruits, cigars, and rice brandy. —*William H. Bishop 1833*

There has been little rest for the dead in San Francisco. Russian Hill, the Civic Center, Laurel Heights, the side of Lone Mountain, and Lincoln Park were all the sites of nineteenth-century cemeteries, most vacated under pressure from real estate interests and their occupants moved to Colma in San Mateo County. Pictured above, left, is a remnant of a Chinese cemetery hidden among cypresses on Lincoln Park Golf Course. Much of the granite masonry from the former clifftop cemeteries can still be seen, now lapped by the waves near Land's End.

This beautiful cemetery is located in a northeasterly part of Oakland and is easily reached by the Piedmont street-car line. . . . Its avenues are lined by choice flowers and supplied by beautiful fountains. There are handsome and costly monuments scattered through the grounds. . . .

The plan of Mountain View Cemetery was laid out by Mr. Frederick Law Olmsted, one of the most distinguished experts in landscape gardening, and his recommendations for its improvement and ornamentation are being carried out as nearly as possible. . . .

It is a part of the duty of the Superintendent to explain the plans to persons wanting lots, to give information concerning the choice of trees, their adaptation to the soil, and their arrangement with reference to the landscape. . . .

Entering this broad gateway . . . the road diverges into three separate avenues, the one on the left leading to the Catholic, the central one to the Hebrew, and the right hand to the Protestant quarter. —*W. W. Elliott c. 1885*

Mountain View Cemetery (above, right) was laid out in 1865, with the attention usually given only to a park, on the lowest slopes of the Oakland Hills. Its designer, Frederick Law Olmsted, bettered San Francisco's desolate, wind-scourged cemetery, which, he noted, was the only place for picnicking in that city.

The train runs through Oakland, a lovely live-oak suburb of San Francisco, thirty thousand strong, where a thousand houses a year has been the recent rate of growth. You catch a glimpse of the tropical glories. You see hedges of fuchsias and walls of scarlet geraniums twelve feet high. . . . You see walls of evergreen carved into arches and alcoves and gateways . . . calla lilies as large and pure as holy chalices.
—*Benjamin Taylor 1870s*

Oakland, named after its groves of live oak, claimed itself to be more healthful than San Francisco on account of its spaciousness and better climate and sewer system. It was free of the industries that hung a pall of smoke over San Francisco but benefited economically from being the terminus of the transcontinental railroad. This 1868 Italianate house at Eleventh and Castro streets lay four blocks from the line of the first railroad, which pierced the East Bay hills at Niles Canyon in southern Alameda County and ran along Seventh Street in Oakland out to a pier jutting toward Yerba Buena Island. The house was the home of George C. Pardee, mayor of Oakland and later a conservationist governor of California. In the foreground is a water tower (missing its tank) that stored water from the family's well.

If there be any such thing as "the genius of the American people," a phrase which public speakers delight to apply . . . it is chiefly manifested in our capacity for developing a new country. We hate to see lands uncultivated. . . . We praise the man who plants orchards, vineyards, shade-trees, shrubberies, lawns, gardens, hedges and small fruits. —*Charles H. Shinn 1879*

Opposite: Gardening was a highly fashionable and sentimental activity in the Victorian era, when a blooming rarity such as the giant waterlily *Victoria amazonica* in Golden Gate Park was the talk of the town. Since that time, new fashions and neglect have obliterated all planting patterns favored by earlier generations except for the trees: palms, cedars, the California pepper (originating in Peru), elm, acacia, and black locust. The South African calla lilies seen opposite have been a perpetual favorite since pioneer days; other flowers popular in early San Francisco were the oleander, rose, camellia, lemon verbena, hollyhock, and dahlia. One of California's earliest nurserymen was James Shinn, who in 1876 moved into this, his new farmhouse, in Fremont. To the left of the house is a notable recent planting: the dawn redwood (*Metasequoia glyptostroboides*), an ancestor of the coast redwood believed long extinct until it was found in 1945 by Chinese biologists in Sichuan Province. James Shinn's son, Charles, was a prolific writer and promoter of conservative forestry management.

A woman who is the owner of ten acres, two acres of orchard, and devotes eight acres more to grass, flowers and poultry, will find that all the plowing, cultivating, pruning, woodsawing and heavy lifting can be done by one [hired] man in a part of the year; that picking, drying and packing fruit, gathering nuts, making jellies, preserving and canning fruits and vegetables during one season of the year; and milking one or two cows, making butter and raising poultry as a principal business the rest of the year, is easier, pleasanter, and more healthful than any city employment. Then, when the year's work is done, and no special disaster has interfered with success, two or three thousand dollars clear profit feels much more satisfactory in the pocket than the savings of a weekly earnings behind the counter, the case, the desk or the sewing machine. —*California, Home for the Emigrant 1878*

The virgin soils of California's temperate valleys produced miraculous crops. Some settlers, however, bought land in the blush of springtime, only to find that summer turned their homestead into a parched and lifeless holding. The California Immigrant Union in its publication *California, Home for the Emigrant* promised easy success to women in farming, a progressive view for the 1870s—or perhaps merely a ploy by which another easterner could be tempted to California. February plowing has begun on the ranch seen above near Fremont in Alameda County.

Fourteen big ships are lashed to the warehouse docks at Port Costa, and two hundred sturdy men are loading the Fair Syndicate wheat for Liverpool. It is a large lot—180,000 tons in all—and fills the spacious warehouses to overflowing. . . . This year's crop will begin to come in about the last week in June, and where it is to be stored is what nobody seems to know. . . .

Port Costa is a quiet town with a fluctuating population. For nine months in the year she dreams in languorous inactivity. There is little toil, and no spinning to speak of. But when the hills above the town grow bare and brown, the long wheat trains rumble in from the valleys of the south, and the town bestirs itself from a nine months' lethargy, and takes on a boom aspect. —*San Francisco Daily Morning Call 1895*

The town of Port Costa, nestled in a valley on the south side of Carquinez Strait, was the major shipping point for California's wheat, and from the 1880s until World War I went through a yearly cycle of boom and bust. Barges and trains brought the harvest from north and south—the San Joaquin Valley was the largest producer—and at the height of the wheat trade, several hundred square riggers, mostly British, could be seen at once in San Francisco Bay waiting to load a millon-ton harvest. The major part of the harvest went to England, the rest to Southern Europe, Australia, and China. One of these ships, *Balclutha,* still rides the bay, moored permanently at San Francisco's National Maritime Museum.

The tall straw, nearly four feet high, was perfectly straight, and the compact growth of the ears rendered it impossible for the heavier to droop. When threshed, almost every grain in the immense field was of the same size and color, pale and plump, as good California wheat always is. This grain farm gives employment to 60 men, 140 horses and mules; uses three herders, five reaping machines, and two steam threshers. In the ploughing season, eighty acres are ploughed, sowed, and harrowed, daily. —*Titus Fey Cronise 1867*

Wheat, introduced by missionaries, then neglected during the Gold Rush, became California's major export crop in the latter part of the nineteenth century. Mild winters and warm summers often enabled farmers to harvest two crops of wheat from the same ground in a year. In the 1860s, the Santa Clara Valley yielded twenty-five to thirty bushels an acre every year without fertilizers or irrigation. Other productive farms lay in the Livermore Valley, where in 1867 agricultural author Titus Fey Cronise noted the remarkable fertility of the soil. California wheat was very dry when harvested, so had the great advantage of not suffering mildew damage on the long sea journeys to foreign markets.

Twenty years ago a ride through this section was practically a trip through an enormous wheat field, broken here and there by a vine-yard or a market garden. Today one sees miles on miles of wheat, but even the very large fields are dwarfed by the thousands of acres in fruit and vines. The old order has changed; the great wheat ranch has given place to the small fruit farm; a hundred substantial homes now dot the plain where once the steam plow turned its ten-mile furrows and the great harvester marked its progress across fields as large as Eastern counties by long lines of well-filled wheat sacks. —*George H. Fitch 1880s*

Eventual soil exhaustion in the Santa Clara Valley was in large part responsible for the transformation from wheat farms to orchard trees with their deeper-reaching roots. The French prune was introduced by Louis Pellier in the late 1850s and in twenty years was the main orchard crop in the valley. Ever larger acreages were planted to orchard trees, whose crop was packed off to the East, and in the 1920s and 1930s tourists from all over the Bay Area rode down in their automobiles to view the blossoms of nine million prune, plum, cherry, and almond trees filling "The Valley of Heart's Delight" from side to side. Today the scene has changed again, to the industrial parks and suburban housing of "Silicon Valley," and one has to search to find a single commercial orchard. Seen here are cherries near Santa Teresa Boulevard in the southern Santa Clara Valley.

When the planter resolves to plant a vineyard, he should determine whether he is planting to produce grapes for wine or for market. If for the former, he must look for a soil which is made by volcanic eruptions containing red clay and soft rocks, which will decay by exposure to the air. The more magnesia, lime, or chalk the soil contains, so much the better. This kind of soil never cracks, and retains the moisture during the summer admirably. Such a soil will produce a wine that will keep good for fifty or one hundred years, and improve annually; is not liable to get sour, or when exposed to the air after one year old, to get turbid, and change color in the bottle or glass.
—*Agoston Haraszthy 1862*

The enterprising Hungarian Agoston Haraszthy is credited with founding the California wine industry. Spanish vines were cultivated at the missions, and General Vallejo produced wines at Sonoma, but Haraszthy was the first to plant large acreages. After a failure in San Mateo County, in 1856 he moved to Sonoma Valley, where he found native grape vines growing vigorously. A

sweet-scented blossom of *Vitis californica* is pictured at left. In 1862 Haraszthy had three hundred acres near Sonoma planted in vines, including Tokay, Zinfandel, and Persian Shiras varieties, and was constructing cellars and a press house (seen above) with rock excavated from hillside tunnels. Hundreds more varieties were added to California's stock following his state-commissioned trip to Europe, but he was most successful with Zinfandel and Muscat, well suited to local soils and climate. Below are seventy-year-old Carignane vines putting out their first leaves of the year in Uvas Valley ("grapes" valley in Spanish), Santa Clara County. Haraszthy's cellars are still in use, part of the modern Buena Vista Winery (the name of Haraszthy's original operation), but the tunnels collapsed in the 1906 earthquake. There is a chance that the tunnels still hold Haraszthy's vintages and that their keeping qualities will one day be put to the test.

W e were shown a map giving subterranean topography of this mine; and truly, the crossings and recrossings, the windings and intricacies of the labyrinthine passages could only be compared to the streets of a dense city. . . . The miners have named the different passages after their saints, and run them off as readily as we do the streets of a city; and after exhausting the names of all the saints in the calendar, have commenced on different animals, one of which is not inaptly called *el Elefante*. Some idea of the extent and number of these passages may be formed, when we state, that sixty pounds of candles are used by the workmen in the twenty-four hours. —*S. A. Downer 1870*

The New Almaden quicksilver mine in Santa Clara County produced a mercury supply indispensable in the refining of gold ore, and in fact its yield had a higher value than any California gold mine. It was probably also the longest-operating mine in California, for Indians extracted the ore, cinnabar, for body decoration, and from the 1820s Mexicans attempted to reduce the ore to silver and gold. Around the period of American annexation, the true nature of the ore was discovered, and Hispanic and English miners—living in separate camps—were hired to systematically mine the area. Ultimately over a hundred miles of passages were dug beneath the wooded hills and reached six hundred feet below sea level before New Almaden finally closed in the 1970s. The land is now a county park, but, as a legacy of the past, mercury continues to wash into the creeks and reservoirs, rendering fish poisonous.

Opposite: In the Bay Area, an age-old method of collecting salt from evaporation ponds has expanded into an industry that today circulates the salty solution in a five-year journey around ponds covering fifty square miles of bayshore. The dry summer, ocean breeze, large flat shore, and clay soil beneath the ponds are exploited by Leslie Salt to harvest over a million tons of crude salt a year. Inset is a storage pile at the Port of Redwood City. In the early days of American California, bay salt was used for preserving fish and was quite unpalatable for home use because of impurities. Now this salt has a myriad of industrial uses and, refined, fills the kitchen salt shaker.

T he chief occupation of the inhabitants . . . is the collection of salt, which forms in large quantities on the land overflowed by the waters of the bay, and affords employment to some 150 men. The quantity of salt collected annually exceeds 10,000 tons. . . . The whole of it is collected and purified by solar evaporation. The salt water is retained in reservoirs, during high tides, and evaporated in shallow ponds ranging in size from twenty to five hundred acres. Some of these salt ponds— mostly formed of earth—are located in swamps, which though a few years since deemed absolutely worthless, are now valued at from four to ten dollars per acre. —*Titus Fey Cronise 1867*

Marin County offers some important advantages to the dairy farmer. The sea-fogs which it receives cause abundant springs of excellent soft water, and also keep the grass green through the summer and fall in the gulches and ravines. . . . The county is full of dairy farms, and as this business requires rather more and better buildings than wheat, cattle or sheep farming, as well as more fences, this gives the country a neater and thriftier appearance than is usual among farming communities in California. —*Charles Nordhoff 1874*

In the late 1860s Marin dairy farms produced one and a half million pounds of butter annually—more than any other county in California—shipping it by schooner from Tomales Bay to San Francisco. The Pierce Ranch below, far out on the windy Point Reyes Peninsula, was the largest producer, with 250 cows. Bought by Solomon Pierce in 1858, the ranch remained in the family for three generations, and its buildings are now preserved as part of the Point Reyes National Seashore. Dairying continues elsewhere within the park and is still the major agricultural activity of Marin and the third largest agricultural producer in the Bay Area after flowers and grapes.

Strangers visiting Oakland and Alameda notice graceful trees standing much higher than any of the ancient oaks. These are the famous eucalypti, which although planted only ten or twelve years ago, have shot up into young giants. Some of these are 70 ft. high, measuring seven feet eight inches in circumference, three feet above ground. . . . Some of the timber was shown to a carpenter, who after a deliberate examination, pronounced it hickory, having all the toughness and, as the carpenter expressed it, "cheesey cut" of the best ash or white oak.

There is nothing, unless it is a mortgage on one's homestead, that grows as fast as a eucalyptus, and it is not improbable that a well-planted grove of them would overtake and capture the mortgagor. . . . It bids fair to be of the greatest value to California, which has much need of a timber suitable for wagons and machinery. —*California, Home for the Emigrant 1878*

Zealous promotion of the practical uses of the eucalyptus, an Australian native, led to massive plantings undertaken from the 1870s up to about 1910. The fast-growing tree was claimed to drive away malaria and provide useful oils and excellent wood for furniture and fuel. Hundreds of miles of eucalyptus were planted as windbreaks for the citrus groves of southern California. There are over five hundred species,

and unfortunately their differing characteristics were too often ignored, with the result that the whole genus fell into disrepute except as an ornamental. Pictured here is a grove of blue gum (*Eucalyptus globulus*), planted on the Berkeley campus of the University of California in 1877, four years after the university moved from Oakland. Today these fragrant trees have reached a height of nearly two hundred feet.

Woodside, about six miles from Redwood City, though it makes no pretensions to the title of town or village, is nonetheless somewhat of a public place. Situated at the foot of the mountains, in the immediate vicinity of several mills, it is the center of quite a trade. It has one store in which is the post-office. Mountain Dell Division No. 74, Sons of Temperance, is located here. At this point, also, the citizens have done what has not been accomplished in any other place in the county — they have formed a library association, and have already accumulated quite an extensive library of excellent works. —*San Mateo County Gazette 1859*

Overleaf: The Woodside Store, built in 1854, five years after the first sawmills were set up in the nearby valleys, served the loggers of the then-remote region, and storekeeper Robert O. Tripp was also their dentist. The wood was nearly gone by the late 1860s, and the store began to supply the farmers of the cleared land. The building is now preserved as a county museum.

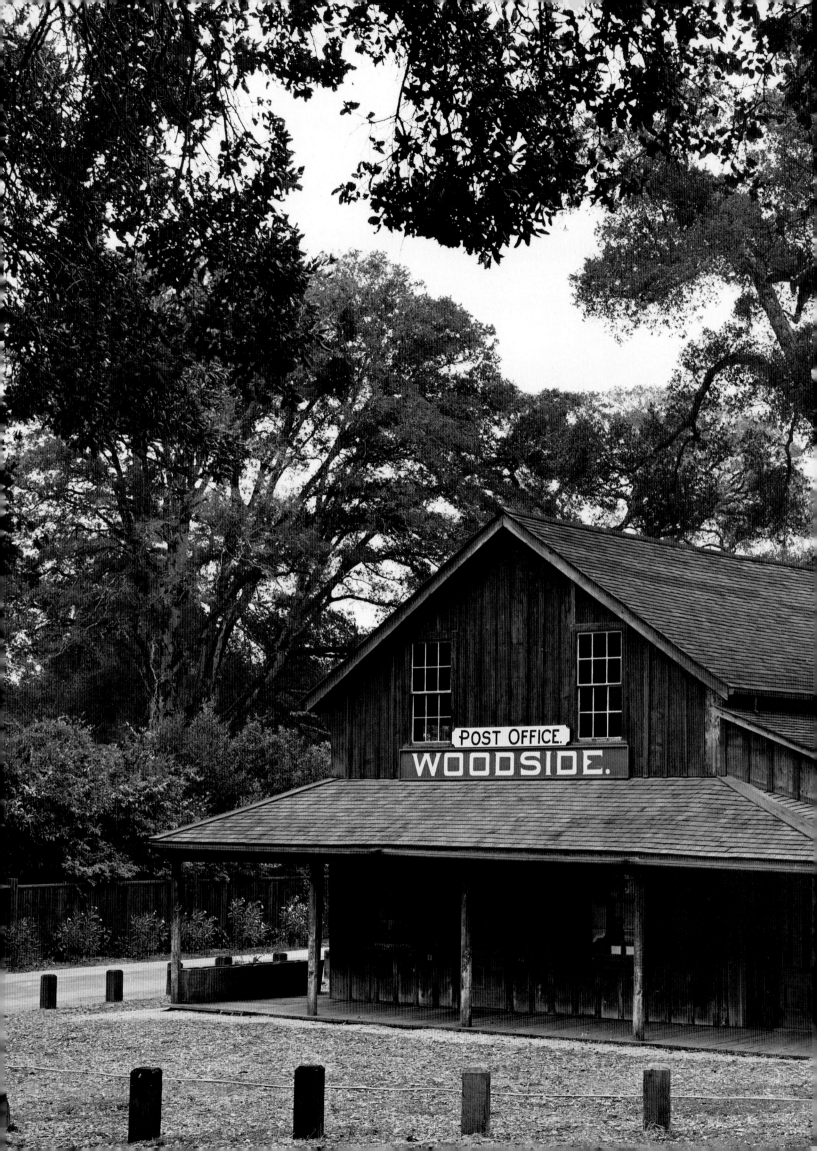

The whole building from foundation to roof (excepting floor) was built from the product of one Redwood tree. This tree stood near Guerneville in the county of Sonoma, and was sawed into lumber by the late Rufus Murphy. It yielded 78,000 feet of lumber, of which 57,000 feet was clear of knots. A portion of the top of the tree was broken and shattered in the fall of the tree, and for that reason was made into shingles. . . . This was done . . . first, as an advertisement for his mill, and second, to show the marvelous product of one of California's trees. — *T. J. Butts 1900*

The First Baptist Church of Santa Rosa was built from a single redwood tree in 1874. Apparently the mill owner failed to publicize the feat, and word of the Gothic-style church's unusual origin only spread at the turn of the century, when the affidavit of T. J. Butts, one of the mill workers, was recorded. In 1957 the building was moved half a mile to its present location adjacent to Juilliard Park and now houses the Robert Ripley Believe It or Not Museum, named after the cartoonist native to Santa Rosa.

The stony trunks lying in woodland north of Santa Rosa are evidence that giant redwood trees grew in this region long before many of the prominent features of today's landscape were formed. In the late Pliocene epoch, some two or three million years ago, volcanos erupted in the area of Sonoma, Napa, and Lake counties, and the lava flows, since shifted and eroded into new patterns, now make up the mountains of Saint Helena, Cobb, and Boggs. Many redwoods were flattened during the eruptions and blanketed with ash, preventing decomposition. Over the following thousands of years, the wood was replaced, little by little, by silicates. Now uncovered by erosion and man's hand, each petrified tree is a perfect replica of its fibrous original.

What a rocking of the cradle there must have been when the earth quaked, and lava put these trees in flinty armor and transfused their veins with dumbness! . . . They overwhelm your vanity with grey cairns of what once danced in the rain, whispered in the wind, blossomed in the sun. — *Benjamin Taylor 1870s*

The whole neighborhood of Mount Saint Helena is full of sulphur and of boiling springs. . . . Hot Springs and White Sulphur Springs are the names of two stations on the Napa Valley Railroad; and Calistoga itself seems to repose on a mere film above a boiling, subterranean lake. . . . It keeps this end of the valley as warm as toast. I have gone across to the hotel a little after five in the morning, when a sea-fog from the Pacific was hanging thick and grey, and dark and dirty overhead, and found the thermometer had been up before me, and had already climbed among the nineties. —*Robert Louis Stevenson 1880*

Scottish author Robert Louis Stevenson and his bride Fanny spent part of their honeymoon in Calistoga. The resort town at the head of Napa Valley was created by pioneer capitalist Sam Brannan for the relaxation of San Franciscans and is dominated by massive Mount Saint Helena. Today, resort hotels still tap the hot springs, fired by the molten rock of the earth's interior some five miles down, and the Old Faithful Geyser of California (pictured here) spouts about once an hour, attracting visitors with time on their hands. On the other side of the mountain, the once-famous Geysers, the "Gates of Hell," are now harnessed and meet the energy needs of one and a half million people.

The lawn . . . is surrounded by a system of little five-roomed cottages, each with a verandah and a weedy palm before the door. Some of the cottages are let to residents, and these are wreathed in flowers. The rest are occupied by ordinary visitors to the hotel; and a very pleasant way this is, by which you have a little country cottage of your own, without domestic burthens, and by the day or week. —*Robert Louis Stevenson 1880*

At its height, Brannan's Calistoga Springs included about twenty cottages, bath and pool, observatory, winery, stable, and race track. The picturesque cottage shown above, built in 1866, is one of two that remain. Its "weedy palm"—as Stevenson described it—now towers over the house on Wapoo Avenue (named after the local Indian tribe), opposite Pacheteau's Hot Springs.

A long the unfenced, abominable mountain roads, he launches his team with small regard to human life or the doctrine of probabilities. Flinching travellers, who behold themselves coasting eternity at every corner, look with natural admiration at the driver's huge, impassive, fleshy countenance. — *Robert Louis Stevenson 1880*

The shortest stage route climbing northwest over the rugged Mayacmas Mountains between Calistoga and the Geysers was built in the 1860s by Clark Foss, a famous and corpulent driver who also ran a stage to the Petrified Forest. Foss made the twenty-six-mile journey one too many times: an accident threw his 265-pound frame off the coach, fatally injuring him. Seen above is the road's approach to a sharp bend named Cape Horn by the residents of now-vanished Pine Flat, a mercury mining town. On the extreme left of the photograph is Mount Saint Helena; at its foot is the fog-filled Napa Valley.

[F]elton's new bridge] rests like an eagle on tip of wings, upon two mighty concrete pillars, one on either side of the famous San Lorenzo River as the rushing waters roll beneath it. . . . No longer will the water roll into your buggy as you cross the river, nor will others be required to stand on their heads as the horse becomes frightened at the water and runs from under them, nor yet have occasion to be dumped in the surf as the girth breaks and the cart upsets. — *Santa Cruz Surf 1892*

Felton, in the Santa Cruz Mountains, sprang up as a lumber town and boomed in the 1870s. Its redwood covered bridge — built in 1892 and one of only three old covered bridges remaining in the Bay Area — supported a traffic of stagecoaches and carts loaded with apples, apricots, prunes, and cherries making their way to Santa Cruz. Later it carried automobiles and trucks up until 1938, when it was bypassed. The roof and siding have served for many years to protect the structural elements from weather damage.

On the Threshold

*We are not building this country of ours for a day. It is to last
through the ages. We stand on the threshold of a new century. . . .
If we are true . . . the generations that succeed us here shall
fall heir to a heritage such as has never been known before.*

The San Franciscan of 1906 looking to the
future from the rubble of a destroyed city.

By the 1890s the Bay Area's profligate youth was over.
Frontier life was finished, San Francisco had become
big and dirty, and Oakland was suffering growing pains;
the productivity of the region's soil and mines was
diminishing.

A new reflective spirit was affecting the nation and locally
found clear expression in three architectural developments. Most
dramatic was the City Beautiful movement, inspired by ancient
classical and Renaissance models and advocating large-scale city
planning with broad boulevards and parks. An ambitious plan
for a new San Francisco was presented to the city supervisors on
the eve of the 1906 earthquake, and as if to order, fire obliterated
the whole center of the Victorian city; but it could not erase the
property lines, and owners were impatient to rebuild the city on
its old pattern. The plan was shelved, except for those pages with
sketches for a new civic center. If in 1906 San Francisco was
demolished and a grand plan was not given its day, in the city's
Panama-Pacific International Exposition of 1915, a grand plan
was given its day only to be demolished. A reconstruction of one
of the exposition's buildings, the Palace of Fine Arts, remains, a
reminder of a bold gesture of bravura.

Plates fused in the fire of 1906

A second movement, also retrospective in character, cen-
tered on a newfound appreciation of California's architectural
heritage: the crumbled mission buildings and Fort Ross were
restored or reconstructed as part of a past being rapidly obscured.
In the old adobes, the Mission Revival and Spanish styles in new
architecture found their beginnings, to be popularized in the San
Diego Exposition of 1915.

Thirdly, the First Bay Tradition and closely related Crafts-
man style, a new trend in local architecture, decried Victorian

Sculpture from the Golden Gate
International Exposition, 1939

commercialism and the defacing of nature. Favoring local materials and using the natural features of the site, private houses were made as inconspicuous as possible.

Increasing numbers of critical voices were protesting what mankind was doing with its mechanical might. Natural resources—minerals, forests, wildlife, groundwater, and soil fertility—were being rapidly used up as if there were a new frontier ahead. In the Bay Area, conservationist groups such as the Sierra Club and Sempervirens Club (now Sempervirens Fund) were formed and found a receptive ear in President Theodore Roosevelt. Public pressure for parkland resulted in the creation of the first state redwood preserve, Santa Cruz County's Big Basin, in 1902, and in the formation of the East Bay Regional Park District in 1933.

This era saw the invention of the biggest boon and the biggest bane of the Bay Area: the automobile. In the early years of this century, the first autos were restricted to a speed of four miles an hour around corners and had to stop for horses, but in twenty years the automobile was king of the road. It opened up the region's hinterlands to sightseers and the fields for homesites. With the opening of the Bay Bridge in 1936 and the Golden Gate Bridge in 1937, tides of commuters were set free to cover the whole of the San Francisco Bay Area. ⁊

Alameda County Court House, a Works Progress Administration project

Bay Bridge, view west to San Francisco

Joaquin Miller Park, Oakland

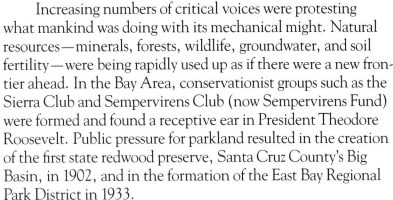

Colma, San Mateo County

At . . . the Palo Alto Rancho . . . we shall find the home and training-ground of some of California's most noted racers, as well as the training-ground of California's sturdy sons and daughters; for here, . . . fast drawing toward the opening day, is the Cambridge of the west, the truly magnificent Leland Stanford, Jr. University. If the Palo Alto Rancho succeeds in training young humanity half as well as she has heretofore trained her blooded horses and her thoroughbreds, she may indeed rest contented on her well-earned laurels. . . . The architecture is highly appropriate and characteristic of California, following as far as possible the style of the churches and buildings of the early missionary Fathers. The main court is already completed. —*Albert Gray 1888*

Stanford University was built as a memorial to the teenage son of Senator Leland Stanford, former president of the Central Pacific Railroad. Stanford, by incorporating features of mission architecture in the design, believed he was fostering a regional architecture appropriate to a fully emancipated state. However, the design owes as much to Richardsonian Romanesque, the favored style of the project's three Boston architects, Shepley, Rutan, and Coolidge. The new university opened in 1891, and parts of the campus suffered considerable earthquake damage in 1906.

There are some six hundred horses to provide for, and each has its separate stall. . . . The stock farm is provided with everything that is needed, including a blacksmith shop, a wheelwright shop, and a mill to grind feed. There are fifty paddocks of three acres each for grazing purposes. At night all are under shelter, except that some of the older animals are left out during the summer. —*Hubert Howe Bancroft 1880s*

Leland Stanford founded his immaculately kept horse farm as a relaxation from his railroad interests, but it soon became the largest in the world. He intended to contribute to the health of the nation's economy (in a preautomobile world) by improving horsebreeding and became involved in original and successful techniques for producing record-breaking trotters. The Red Barn (pictured), built in about 1878, was the largest of a spread of nine stables and barns. Here Edweard Muybridge conducted many of his horse locomotion studies using ranks of cameras, experiments that led to the development of motion pictures. Today, much of the farm has been turned over to other uses by Stanford University, but the barn remains in use as a riding stable.

The profession of mining has to do with the very body and bone of the earth, its process is a ruthless assault upon the bowels of the world, a contest with the most rudimentary forces. There is something about it essentially elementary, something primordial, and its expression in architecture must be true and have something of the rude, the Cyclopean. The emotion raised must be one of power, not grace.

Even the scale of materials, the blocks of stone of which the walls are built, should be bolder and more strongly masculine than that of any other structure. —*John Galen Howard 1902*

The imposing steel-frame and granite Hearst Memorial Mining Building, designed for the University of California at Berkeley by John Galen Howard, was part of the university's ambitious new construction program, inspired by the 1893 Chicago Columbian Exhibition. During the first two decades of this century, massive classical buildings in the Beaux Arts tradition— fifteen of them designed by Howard—were set in an informal landscape laid out at the foot of the Berkeley Hills. Much of the landscaping has since been lost under newer construction. The building pictured is a memorial to Senator George Hearst, who made a fortune in gold, silver, and copper mining and went on to found the *San Francisco Examiner,* still in Hearst hands today.

In the early morning the city was almost noiseless. Occasionally a newspaper wagon clattered up the street or a milk wagon rumbled along. One of my companions had told a funny story. We were laughing at it. We stopped—the laugh unfinished on our lips.

Of a sudden we had found ourselves staggering and reeling. It was as if the earth was slipping gently from under our feet. Then came a sickening swaying of the earth that threw us flat upon our faces. We struggled in the street. We could not get on our feet.

I looked in a dazed fashion around me. I saw for an instant the big buildings in what looked like a crazy dance. Then it seemed as though my head were split with the roar that crashed into my ears. Big buildings were crumbling as one might crush a biscuit in one's hand. Great gray clouds of dust shot up with flying timbers, and storms of masonry rained into the street. Wild, high jangles of smashing glass cut a sharp note into the frightful roaring. Ahead of me a great cornice crushed a man as if he were a maggot, a laborer in overalls on his way to the Union Iron Works, with a dinner pail on his arm. —*P. Barrett 1906*

Plans for the greater, the new San Francisco are rapidly taking shape, and out of the chaos of shattered buildings and broken fortunes, above the charred fragments of the once proud metropolis will rise the new city by the western sea, the home of the strongest, bravest, and sturdiest people of their race. —*San Francisco Bulletin, April 21, 1906*

The time was 5:13 A.M., April 18, 1906, and the earth was stirring. Lasting for forty-eight seconds, the earthquake would have registered about 8.3 on the Richter Scale. The masonry buildings—concentrated in the downtown area—and their occupants suffered most from the earth movement. Ninety percent of the city consisted of wood-frame buildings, and these rode through the jolting relatively unscathed, except for ones built on soft ground. But the wooden buildings were helpless before the fires that started when gas lines ruptured. Fire engines found themselves without a water supply. Over two thousand people died as a result of the earthquake. The Flood Building (pictured) on Market Street, a luxurious and newly completed steel-frame structure at the time of the earthquake, survived the shaking but was gutted by fire at the end of the first day.

Over four and a half square miles of San Francisco were destroyed in the 1906 earthquake, from the Embarcadero west to Van Ness Avenue, and south to China Basin and nearly to Mission Dolores. The memorial to iron-founder Peter Donahue shown below was erected in 1894 and survived the quake when all around it fell. Today it still stands at Market and Battery streets as a witness to the ambitiousness and fragility of mankind's creations. Many other monumental sculptures came through unscathed but were moved to Golden Gate Park during the 1940s to make room for the automobile. Rubble was carried away on railcars and horsecarts, constant work that cost the lives of fifteen thousand horses. Within three years the city was largely rebuilt, but by this time many of its citizens had resettled permanently in the East Bay and on the San Francisco Peninsula, stimulating the growth of other communities.

o his eyes yearn for a sight of Chinatown that lay in the heart of the business district like a piece of rare old cloisonné on a square of grey cloth? He can find consolation in the thought that it is all to be rebuilt in the Oriental style of architecture, and that it will probably not be long ere the newness wears off, and it will again take on the rich hues of the famous quarter. —*Elizabeth Haight Strong 1906*

The pre-1906 Chinatown, of simple wooden houses with Chinese embellishments, was already a tourist destination. The new, more fireproof Chinatown was rebuilt of brick within two years, with far more ornate cornicework, the better to lure visitors, but Chinatown is now considered a serious earthquake hazard.

I nternational expositions . . . are phantom kingdoms wherein
the people do everything but sleep. . . . Their magic growth
is similar to the mushroom and moonflower, they vanish like
setting suns in their own radiance. . . . The National Constitu-
tion of phantom kingdoms commands that the Spirit of beauty,
refinement, education, culture and frolic shall govern. The result
is that they contain many palaces and shrines decorated with
sculpture and painting, and that the earth is studded with fountains and pools within tropical gardens. Such a kingdom exists

Architects, poets, and politicians all waxed ecstatic over the Panama-Pacific International Exposition, held in 1915 on newly made land on San Francisco's northern shore. Louis Mullgardt, designer of a score of houses and public buildings in the Bay Area, was its chief architect. The opening of the Panama Canal and the spirit of internationalism brought with it, together with the rapid rebuilding of San Francisco, put the population in high spirits. All that remains of the 635-acre exposition is the reconstructed Palace of Fine Arts (pictured), designed by Bernard Maybeck.

within a wonderful valley bordering on a great sea. It is surrounded by high velvet hills of fine contour and by many real
cities. As the people look down on this phantom kingdom from
the hilltops, or from ships sailing on the water, they see Architecture nestling like flamingos with fine feathers unfurled within a
green setting. . . . Architecture and the sister arts are the most
reliable barometers in recording human thought. They are direct
exponents of a universal language wherein national progress is
most clearly read. —*Louis Christian Mullgardt 1915*

L A N D M A R K S

Let the work be simple and genuine, with due regard to right proportion and harmony of color. . . . Eliminate in so far as possible all factory-made accessories in order that your dwelling may not be typical of American commercial supremacy, but rather of your own fondness for things that have been created as a response to your love of that which is good and simple and fit for daily companionship. Far better that our surroundings be rough and crude in detail, provided that they are a vital expression conceived as part of an harmonious scheme, than that they be finished with mechanical precision and lacking in genuine character. Beware the gloss that covers over a sham!
—*Charles Keeler 1904*

The rustic brown-shingled studio shown opposite, designed in 1902 by Bernard Maybeck for Berkeley poet, esthete, and ornithologist Charles Keeler, stands in reaction to the showiness of Victorian mansions. Keeler promoted a characteristic Bay Area architecture, now known as the First Bay Tradition, recognizable by its use of natural-looking local materials, handcrafted work, and respect for the natural features of the landscape. Many such houses are found in north Berkeley, designed by Maybeck, Julia Morgan, and Ernest Coxhead.

The Pulgas Water Temple, dedicated in 1934, marks the spot near Woodside where the 163-mile aqueduct from Hetch Hetchy in Yosemite National Park reaches San Francisco's storage reservoir, Crystal Springs, in San Mateo County. The damming of the Tuolumne River in 1923 was effected in the face of great opposition from environmentalists such as John Muir, the voluble spokesman for a wilderness preservation movement reacting against the overcivilization of the American. The movement's underlying philosophy harked back to Thoreau and other nineteenth-century Transcendentalists. Supporters of the dam, such as city supervisor Phil Katz, promoter of a bond issue to complete the aqueduct, compared the engineering feat to the city's rebuilding after the 1906 earthquake in terms of magnitude and importance. The temple's inscription, from Isaiah 43:20, reads, "I give waters in the wilderness and rivers in the desert to give drink to my people."

All this greatness and prosperity which are heralding to the world, our growing bank clearings, our building boom, our increasing population, our development of more shipping from this port will come to naught unless this city can guarantee to its population and to the people and commerce that is coming here a plentiful supply of pure water at low rates. Only by the completion of the Hetch Hetchy can this supply be insured. —*Phil Katz 1924*

These temple destroyers, devotees of ravaging commercialism, seem to have a perfect contempt for Nature, and instead of lifting their eyes to the God of the Mountains, lift them to the Almighty Dollar. —*John Muir 1912*

The future of California depends upon the conservation of its water supply. Without this the land will become a desert. The forests are the only power which can restrain the impatient torrents from despoiling the land—from rushing down the mountains in freshets and tearing away the soil of the valleys. —*Charles Keeler 1903*

These eight-foot-deep erosion gorges were carved by rain and rivulets into a hillside in Point Richmond, Contra Costa County, after removal of the plant cover that normally stabilizes the soil with its roots and releases excess water gradually. The mountains of the Coast Ranges—and later the Sierra Nevada—became increasingly important as water catchment areas when the Bay Area's population grew too large to be supplied solely by wells and local creeks. Heavy logging of the mountains jeopardized the usefulness of catchment areas by causing flash floods and the siltation of rivers and reservoirs. To guard the water supply, Charles Keeler and others proposed the creation of a string of redwood parks along the coast north to Oregon.

This generation will have for one thing at least a great name in history. Men of the future centuries will surely call it the generation of the great destroyers, and historians and economists will write of the riotous days of nineteen hundred, when the people used up all the petroleum, all the natural gas, all the anthracite and most of the other coal, and most of the handy iron. It will be the period when the forests were cut down or burnt up, the lands stolen, and the waters given away. We are sure to be the subject of earnest remark. —*Benjamin Ide Wheeler 1900s*

There, even while I speak, the axman stands ready to strike. If he pauses, it is only to await your decision. Two years from now his work will be done and the last remaining fragment of the primeval trees which clothe the mountains rising up at the very threshold of our metropolis will have vanished. Vain then, will be our regrets. . . . Were a convulsion of nature to rend in twain and topple over the majestic dome which the genius of Michael Angelo has uplifted above the basilica of Saint Peter, [this] intelligent labor and patience might in time restore. But it is not so here. Man's work, if destroyed, man may again replace. God's work God alone can recreate. Accede then, to the prayers of the people. Save this forest. Save it now. The present generation approves the act; generations yet unborn in grateful appreciation of your labors will rise to consecrate its consummation. —*Delphin M. Delmas 1901*

A disused rock-crusher (opposite) stands starkly against the sky at a Richmond quarry. Benjamin Ide Wheeler, president of the University of California (1899–1919), and others protested against the profligate use of natural resources. United States president Theodore Roosevelt, too, was trying to slow down resource exploitation in California. By the century's first decade, the Bay Area's redwood forests were nearly all gone, most of the coal and mercury mines had closed, and natural gas retrieval in Solano County and oil production in Santa Clara and San Mateo counties required deeper and deeper drilling.

The coast redwood, cousin to the giant sequoia of the Sierra Nevada, is native only to a thirty-mile-wide foggy coastal strip reaching from Big Sur northward into Oregon. With a two-thousand-year lifespan, it can reach over 360 feet in height. The tree's size, straight grain, and resistance to termites and rot make it ideal for house construction and fencing. Realizing the danger to the local forests from loggers, the Sempervirens Club (named after the coast redwood, *Sequoia sempervirens*), campaigned for state funding and control to preserve a grove of ancient trees in the Santa Cruz Mountains. San Francisco lawyer Delphin Delmas spoke persuasively and effectively to the state assembly for the purchase of this forest at Big Basin, which in 1902 became the first state redwoods park and now comprises sixteen thousand acres.

A tree,
A rock,
Has perfect poise and content.
There is no pretending to be anything but itself.
In its life,
A life enclosing whole solar systems within the atom,
There is surely a consciousness
Utterly beyond our comprehension.
Some high emotion
Embraces everything in time and space,
Too fine for language or thought.
There is something in the tree,
Or rock,
Of cosmic consciousness,
Which makes its life infinitely rich.

—*Cedric Wright 1935*

I n pursuing the study of any of the universal and everlasting laws of nature, whether relating to the life, growth, structure, and movements of a giant planet, the tiniest plant, or of the psychological movements of the human brain, some conditions are necessary before we can become one of Nature's interpreters or the creator of any valuable work for the world. . . . Preconceived notions, dogmas, and all personal prejudice and bias must be laid aside; listen patiently, quietly, and reverently to the lessons, one by one, which Mother Nature has to teach, shedding light on that which was before a mystery. . . . Accepting truths as suggested, wherever they may lead, then we have the whole universe in harmony with us. . . . At last man has found a solid foundation for science, having discovered that he is part of a universe which is "eternally unstable in form, eternally immutable in substance."—*Luther Burbank 1895*

Crowned by live oaks, Spirit Rock (opposite) lies mysteriously in a field of California buttercups in San Geronimo Valley, Marin County. Reverence for nature and its rejuvenating influence characterized early Sierra Club outings from Bay Area cities—a mood eloquently expressed by Cedric Wright, photographer and poet laureate of the club's annual Sierra "High Trip."

The reverential, almost mystical approach of Santa Rosa "plant wizard" Luther Burbank, whose home is pictured at the left, proved very successful in the manipulation of Mother Nature's ways to produce new varieties of vegetables, fruits, and flowers. In the foreground are prickly pear cactus hybrids (genus *Opuntia*) Burbank developed to be spineless and thus palatable to desert country cattle. It is said that he paid for a house by selling five cactus segments and the rights to their propagation in the Southern Hemisphere. By the time Burbank died in 1926, the town's idol had developed over eight hundred new plant varieties, including the well-known Burbank potato, Santa Rosa plum, and Shasta daisy.

L A N D M A R K S

When the whistle calls the hour for action, the harvesters take their places—the fireman feeds the fire, the sack-sewers spring to their places at the grain chutes, the separator-man grips his lever. The smoke of the engine sends up its splendid swaying plume; the rejoicing steam pants and hisses; the complex machine quivers, stirs, starts. Now the bank of header-knives fly and flash, cutting a swath of thirty-six feet; now the beltings strain and slip and circle in their many orbits. The separator, the agitator, the cylinders, the fan-wheels, the elevators and chaff-carriers—all begin their mysterious babel, creaking, crashing, buzzing, clanging, snarling, snorting, grating, groaning. The ground shakes as though trampled by the feet of the mastodons. —*Edwin Markham 1914*

California, with its heritage of huge Mexican land grants and plentiful horses to harness, pioneered large-scale farm machinery in the nineteenth century. A combine-harvester dating from 1914 is seen opposite. Manufactured by the Harris Company of Stockton, the wooden body once painted pink with floral decorations, the harvester is still in working order. Such a harvester, pulled and drawn by a steam engine, was vividly described by Edwin Markham, who won national recognition for "The Man with the Hoe," a poem portraying the drudgery of manual farm labor.

The poultry farms literally circle the city of Petaluma, forming a veritable amphitheater, divided into farm centers and districts all touching each other in neighborly fashion, and forming one wonderful chicken world. Yet each farm with its broad acres of chicken yards and colony houses, green kale patches and cozy bungalows sitting in the shade of the eucalyptus groves, has a privacy and individuality all its own. Some of the homes topping the gently rolling ground are modern bungalows, others are the colonial type—each one of them electrically connected with lights, telephone and other conveniences of modern homes. Farther out again within a six mile radius of Petaluma are more farms, but more scattered, covering a larger area of rolling hills and valleys with red-roofed bungalows, white sentinel-like windmills, shade trees and the ever-present flocks of white Leghorns. —*Nellie Denman 1919*

Petaluma's poultry industry began in the late 1870s with Lyman Byce's invention of an egg incubator and his introduction of the Italian Leghorn hen, a champion egg-layer, to the Bay Area's favorable climate. Over the next two decades, Petaluma farmers transformed poultry raising from a backyard occupation into a profitable livelihood. Sonoma County became known as "The World's Egg-basket" and shipped eggs as far as Hawaii, New York, and Europe. Shown here is a chicken farm in nearby Novato that has resisted the trend to mechanized feeding and egg production and still uses pre–World War II "colony houses." The Rhode Island Reds, popular in the nineteenth century for eggs and meat, now supply local health food stores wth fertile brown eggs.

Each junk operates a set of nets, thirty to sixty in number, which are set side by side at the bottom of the bay with their larger openings or mouths open to the current. . . . After the nets are all lifted the junk sails back to the dock at its camp, where the catch is carried, Chinese style, to the boiling vat. . . . The shrimps, together with the fish caught with them, are poured in, ten or twelve baskets at a time, and boiled from ten to fifteen minutes. They are then dipped out with a strainer and put into baskets to be carried to the drying ground. . . . When the weather is good the shrimps will dry in about four days, when they are gathered together and rolled with cleated, wooden rollers to break the shells from the meats. The whole mass is then carried to a shed where it is run through a small fanning mill to separate the loose shells [from the shrimp meat].
—N. B. Scofield 1897

The shrimping industry, dominated by Chinese, was an important activity in San Francisco Bay from the 1870s to the 1930s, when a combination of restrictive legislation, pollution, and reduced freshwater inflow caused its demise. At the industry's peak, an annual catch of five thousand tons of shrimp and incidental fish was landed at some thirty bayside settlements, including today's China Camp (pictured), one of seven near San Rafael in Marin County. The main species caught was the three-inch-long *Crangon franciscorum* (seen here), with lesser numbers of two other shrimp species. In addition to processing plants, this settlement had a store, temple, school, and gaming house. The area is now preserved as China Camp State Park, where an old shrimping boat lies on the beach and a few shrimp are sold as fishing bait.

The west wind ruffles my thin gauze clothing.
On the hill sits a tall building with a room of
wooden planks.
I wish I could travel on a cloud far away,
reunite with my wife and son.
When the moonlight shines on me alone, the
nights seem even longer.
At the head of the bed there is wine and my
heart is constantly drunk.
There is no flower beneath my pillow and
my dreams are not sweet.
To whom can I confide my innermost feelings?
I rely solely on close friends to relieve my loneliness.

—Chinese immigrant

Between 1910 and 1940, Angel Island's North Garrison was used as an immigration station where tens of thousands —mostly Chinese, with smaller numbers of Europeans, Japanese, and other Asians—had to undergo examination and interrogation. Many expressed the loneliness and frustration of their weeks-long stay by writing poems, often marked by a strong sentiment for the natural environment, on the walls of the buildings. Seen here is one of the immigrants' bunkhouses, restored as a feature of Angel Island State Park.

The Packers' ships are northward bound,
There is one that sails today.
Her skipper's got his orders
To proceed to Bristol Bay.
The anchor's up, the topsail's set.
The sky looks kind of murky,
But fair wind or foul, she's coming back
With choice Alaska tyrkey.

—Sea shanty

Each spring between 1893 and 1930, up to thirty square-riggers of the Alaska Packers Association sailed out of the Oakland Estuary, carrying salmon fishermen and cannery workers on the four- to six-week journey to the Bering Sea. The Scottish-built *Balclutha*, named after a town on the River Clyde, was launched in 1886 and in her early years loaded wheat at Port Costa. She later served in the lumber trade across the Pacific before working from 1902 to 1930 as part of the salmon fleet under the name *Star of Alaska*. The steel-hulled ship is now moored at Pier 43 in San Francisco and is open to the public as part of the National Maritime Museum. The rigging design in the illustration of *Star of Alaska* dates from 1909.

Opposite: Drawbridge, on the border between Santa Clara and Alameda counties, grew up alongside a railroad track and took its name from a bridge designed to let boatloads of produce through into the bay. The summer population of vacationers was replaced in the fall by duck hunters arriving on Southern Pacific's Hunters' Special. By 1933 Drawbridge was literally in decline, sinking into the bay because of excessive withdrawal of groundwater from under the Santa Clara Valley. To add to Drawbridge's troubles, encircling salt ponds were being constructed, and pollution made the place less attractive to birds. Now Drawbridge is a ghost town, its few dozen ruins disappearing into the tall bulrushes but protected from vandalism by the San Francisco Bay National Wildlife Refuge.

Drawbridge is one of the few communities in California in which the automobile has never been seen. . . . The reason for this is that the town has no streets. Most of the homes are built on stilts and are connected with board walks. To reach town you have to leave your car in an open field and walk more than two miles across the marsh. —A. J. Petsche 1933

M usic averted panic among 2,000 Marin commuters yesterday when an accident to the machinery of the steamer *Eureka* set the big Northwestern Pacific ferryboat adrift on the bay.

The boat was about two miles out of its slip at Sausalito when the huge walking beam suddenly gave way, due to a broken pin, and crashed through two decks into the engine room.

As a freed connecting rod commenced rending the superstructure with heavy thuds, women screamed and passengers started for the life preservers.

High above the tumult rose a clear tenor voice singing *Marcheta*.

The song dissipated the incipient panic like magic. Unreasoning fear died, life preservers were forgotten and the passengers crowded around the hero of the "shipwreck."

He was Dick Hunter, deckhand, who is widely known in the bay district as "The Caruso of the Ferries." — *San Francisco Examiner 1923*

In 1922 *Eureka* was rebuilt on her thirty-two-year-old hull as the largest passenger ferry in the world, just a year before the *Examiner* reported the dramatic failure of the ship's "walking beam." The beam's diamond-shaped steel frame is seen to the left of the funnel; normally it rocked like a seesaw as it transferred engine power to the paddle wheels (partially visible under the name *Eureka*). Under the ownership of Northwestern Pacific Railway, the 2,300-seat ferryboat ran from Sausalito to San Francisco until 1941, when it was transferred to the Oakland—San Francisco run under Southern Pacific Railroad. Competition from the new bay bridges brought *Eureka* to retirement in 1956 after nearly seven decades of service on the bay, and she is now moored permanently at San Francisco's Hyde Street Pier in the care of the National Maritime Museum.

P rosperity and increase in value are headed this way. The Redwood Highway will become one of the most famous highways in the world. A nation a-wheel will pass this way. And with a Golden Gate Bridge at one end of this road, the world [will] flock to our front yard. — *Sausalito News 1926*

Until the opening of the Golden Gate Bridge, car ferries plied to and from Sausalito, transporting upward of three thousand vehicles on a holiday weekend. Riding on the ferry *Eureka* are: on the right, a 1931 Model A Ford; by its side, a 1924 Dodge Express Wagon; and behind, a 1933 Packard.

At last the mighty task is done;
Resplendent in the western sun
The Bridge looms mountain high,
Its titan piers grip ocean floor,
Its great steel arms link shore with shore,
Its towers pierce the sky.

On its broad decks in rightful pride,
The world in swift parade shall ride,
Throughout all time to be;
Beneath fleet ships from every port,
Vast landlocked bay, historic fort,
And dwarfing all—the sea.

To north, the Redwood Empire's gates;
To south, a happy playground waits,
In Rapturous appeal;
Here nature, free since time began,
Yields to the restless moods of man,
Accepts his bonds of steel.

High overhead its lights shall gleam,
Far, far below life's restless stream,
Unceasingly shall flow;
For this was spun its lithe fine form.
To fear not war, nor time, nor storm.
For Fate had meant it so.

—*Joseph Strauss 1939*

Linking San Francisco with Marin County in 1937, the Golden Gate Bridge was the longest span in the world, with 4,200 feet between its towers. Joseph Strauss, the designer of several hundred bridges, was its chief engineer and au-thor of heroic verses commemorating its open-ing. Strauss became ob-sessed with the gargan-tuan task in 1920 and when it was completed, gave scant recognition to his chief assistant, Clifford Paine, and archi-tect Irving Morrow. Some Marin residents dreaded the accessibility it brought their county, but commuters and Sausalito residents wel-comed the end of daily traffic jams at the ferry terminal. For real estate developers it was a field day. Suddenly the North Bay was within easy reach, and the suburban train system terminating at Sausalito lost its appeal. The daily traffic (both ways) for the first year was nine thousand vehicles. Fifty years later, two hundred thousand vehicles cross each day —and the roadway itself has become the scene of frequent traffic jams.

In Our Hands

A Bay Area scene created by nine- and eleven-year-olds

Saint Francis, by
Beniamino Bufano

I t is impossible to recognize home. I would like to see the preservation of at least the idea [of home], and what keeps the idea alive is the reality of the landscape." The speaker, David Peri—a part-Miwok Indian—and his people struggle to maintain a sense of home while seeing everything of their original land change except the shape of the mountains encircling San Francisco Bay.

Home is the place one considers one's own and where surroundings are familiar, but for Bay Area residents, the dramatic changes that have occurred since the Second World War seem to have left little room for such attachment. For the majority of today's residents—newcomers without extended families nearby to provide a sense of security—things that are constant can be especially valuable. These weathered hills, the native vegetation, and historical landmarks represent an inestimable emotional and psychological value in a changing world.

In just two hundred years the Bay Area's inhabitants have pursued a course from self-sufficiency to a society that has built over the richest soils and is now dependent on outside sources for water, food, energy, and manufactured products—virtually everything except air and cow's milk. Anything can be accomplished with the resources a modern metropolis can command, and the prospect is both exhilarating in its creative potential and cause for misgivings on account of the magnitude of the health- and life-endangering mistakes that can be made. Most perplexing of the questions the region faces are the unpredicted and long-term consequences of human interference with natural processes. Who guessed when water wells were drilled around San Jose that the Santa Clara Valley would eventually sink twenty feet as a result and lead to flooding? The salutary influence of the bay's open water and marshland is now recognized, but what will be

Noe Valley, San Francisco

Wind turbines,
Alameda County

Site of Indian shellmound, Emeryville, Alameda County

50th anniversary of Golden Gate Bridge, 1987

the ultimate effects of toxins now being released into the air and water by industrial and agricultural activities?

Over the past three decades public interest groups have arisen to protect everything that gives the Bay Area its special character: the bay, its water quality and wildlife; the charm of cities on a human scale; open hillsides that provide welcome relief from city life; the area's historical heritage; and a healthful environment that alone has drawn many new residents to California. The preservation movement's results have been impressive. Nearly a million acres of open land are under public ownership, and diverse regional planning authorities are mandated to look beyond short-term economic interests to guard a multitude of other resources. Private agencies and philanthropic individuals with their greater flexibility provide an essential complement to government authorities: they can act quickly to save the habitat of a rare flower, buy a historic mansion, or give a farmer an incentive to stay in business. With any effacement of the Bay Area's natural or man-made blessings, not only are all residents' lives impoverished, but it also can be argued that the accumulated effects of detrimental changes would lead to an irreversible economic decline as the region ceased to attract a talented workforce.

A broad view of the Bay Area is vital to maintaining the quality of life within the region, yet apart from planners and traveling salespeople, few are those who have a sense of the area as a whole. Ultimate responsibility for government and for the support of private agencies remains with the individual resident, whose personal territory extends to, say, half a county only. Perhaps it is in the disparity between the size of the larger unity and that of our personal territories that the problems and solutions of the region lie. They are precious moments when, from an airplane's seat, with a sentimental eye one sees a broad expanse of water and mountains turning beneath and knows that *this* is the San Francisco Bay Area, a happy accident of nature's course, and, to a community of five million people, home. ❧

Surviving coast redwoods

Bayshore sculpture, Alameda County

Summer has slipped by as quietly as can be in a shipyard filled with deafening noise and in a world filled with war. Ships have grown from nothing, slid down the Ways, others have taken their places and taken the graceful plunge too. Our gang works so smoothly now that it is no longer an effort to knock off those steel units faster and faster. The farmers, housewives, salesmen and schoolgirls have learned how to assemble a ship. —*Joseph Fabry 1943*

The United States' entry into World War II in 1941 plunged the San Francisco Bay Area into frenzied activity. Harbor defenses were primed, shipbuilding yards were opened at every practicable port, and war industry workers were attracted from across the country. Liberty ships, such as *Jeremiah O'Brien,* seen here and now moored permanently at Fort Mason's Pier 3 in San Francisco, transported supplies and soldiers to European and Pacific battlefronts.

These vessels were built in an average of six to eight weeks each by work crews with women as a third of the force. The tension and camaraderie of wartime life in the sleepless shipyards of Richmond, a city that quadrupled its population over the war years 1941–1945, has been well told by wartime steelworker Joseph Fabry in his book *Swing Shift.* The Richmond yards launched nearly five hundred ships, and other yards operated at Mare Island, Oakland, Alameda, Sausalito, Hunter's Point in San Francisco, and South San Francisco. During the war, convoys of gray steel carried one and a half million personnel and twenty-three million tons of supplies out through the Golden Gate.

L ittle boxes on the hillside,
Little boxes made of ticky tacky,
Little boxes on the hillside,
Little boxes all the same.
There's a green one and a pink one
And a blue one and a yellow one,
And they're all made out of ticky tacky
And they all look just the same.

— *Malvina Reynolds 1962*

Folksinger Malvina Reynolds's famous song "Little Boxes" was inspired by the monotony of postwar tract housing in Daly City (pictured), built to accommodate disenchanted city-dwellers and an influx of new residents drawn to the Bay Area by the war. Prime mover was developer Henry Doelger, who by 1940 was one of northern California's largest housing contractors, having left his stamp on the Sunset district of San Francisco. In 1945 he bought about 1,350 acres of dunes, cabbage fields, and hog farms resting on the San Andreas fault within today's Daly City and built the community of Westlake. The price was right for the home buyer proud to be living in the suburbs, but subsequently many lawsuits were filed over poor siting, construction, and services. Other complaints against cheaply built tract houses in Hayward, Sunnyvale, and Concord were heard at an exhibition on Bay Area domestic architecture held in 1949, where such housing was compared to the wartime shelters erected for shipyard workers.

The entire valley will be completely urbanized within the next 20 years. It will have been given over to uncontrolled, wasteful urban growth with all its attendant miseries. Its land will have been covered with an unsightly urban mess. Because of the character of the air-drainage basin, which receives the accumulated discharge of the entire San Francisco Bay region under its impenetrable inversion layer, the air-pollution problem is bound to become progressively worse. . . . Roads and freeways already overtaxed will unquestionably become nightmares of traffic. Yet the random development pattern defies solution of its transportation needs by systems of mass and rapid transit. Most important of all for people trapped in this net is the steady erosion of most of the qualities of the environment that only a few years ago made the area an exceedingly attractive place to live. —*Karl Belser 1970*

Mention of the Santa Clara Valley to many Bay Area residents conjures up an image of endless blossoming orchards. The radically altered character of the valley today was anticipated with helpless resignation by Karl Belser, energetic planning director for Santa Clara County from 1950 to 1967. The photograph was taken on a day when a chill north wind swept the valley clear of smog. A similar story may unfold in Alameda County's presently agricultural Livermore Valley, another smog trap, and other parts of the Bay Area where growth is loosely regulated.

Inside this non-stop speedily moving car I felt the road so endless, the distance between places nil, America itself a vast, unobstructed and featureless land full of parallel lines with big circles and curves at intervals, on which masses of colored beetles ran on in endless chain. There were no inhabitants, no shape or form to the hills, mountains and rocks, and all the trees looked like big or small blobs of dark blue or green ink spilt at random. Not a single bird could be seen in flight, for they had become like tiny insects too small to recognize. What has become of man then?—*Chiang Yee 1960s*

Interstate Highway 280, running the length of the San Francisco Peninsula and seen below at its interchange with Highway 92 in San Mateo County, is admired as a masterpiece of engineering for its harmony with the landscape. Freeways nonetheless contribute to the alienation of mankind from nature, a situation lamented by Chinese world traveler and author Chiang Yee.

T his . . . is the record of a search for a special, better way of living. . . . The idea is this: Landscaping offers a way to take house and garden, building materials and plant materials, the open sky and the stars at night, and blend them all to create a deeply satisfying space for everyday living. Through landscaping we are finding a way to make the most of our total environment—nature-created as well as man-made. As housing and stores, schools and industry, freeways and airports absorb more and more of our available "countryside," the opportunity for the individual to renew himself by contact with the natural environment becomes scarcer and scarcer. . . . Close at hand each individual can experience a part of that natural environment most personally. —*Landscaping for Western Living 1958*

Sunset magazine and its associated gardening books revolutionized western suburban living by bringing homeowners out-of-doors and onto patios and shaded decks in planned gardens. Promoting the do-it-yourself approach, *Sunset* books now cover everything from azalea care to weatherstripping. The headquarters (pictured) in Menlo Park, San Mateo County, are open to the public for tours.

Throughout untold millions of years Man has evolved on this planet as a uniquely upright, uniquely clever observer of the natural world. As a result, Man the hunter, the collector, the wanderer, the nest builder, the inventor, artist, and philosopher, has managed to survive fire and flood, tempest and drought, and even the grinding hardship of an ice age that recently brought extinction to many of Earth's creatures.

Still more recently, however, in what amounts to only the barest flicker of evolutionary and geologic time, Man has invented and moved into an environment that is largely of his own making—the modern, industrialized city. And suddenly we are face to face with the possibility that Man may be domesticating himself—losing touch with the great natural realities that have shaped human life throughout the ages. —*Joseph H. Engbeck, Jr. 1980*

From one year's beginning to its end, few of nature's changes are seen in the city: hot and cold, dry and wet describe the seasons. At night, stars and moon are obscured by buildings and street lamps. Parks have become a symbol of nature in an environment where "even trees are put on reservations," as a shocked Native American put it. During the social unrest of the late 1960s, Oakland's youth were bused to the hills in an attempt to defuse animosities, and a new park, Contra Loma, was created for the youth of Contra Costa County. Pictured is San Francisco's Dolores Park, with the downtown in the background.

The closer to the consumer that produce is grown, the better flavor it should have and the fresher it should be — provided that once the grower picks it he doesn't allow it to sit out in the sun. For a small grower to survive and prosper, he should plant those items that the big grower doesn't want to bother with. He'd do well to go into a pick-it-yourself operation. Consumers can find farms in Brentwood and other areas where they can pick their own corn, cucumbers, raspberries and other items. If a grower can provide this service and let people know when to come and pick their own, he's going to do business. There are a lot of families who want to make these trips to the farm to pick, for example, vine-ripened tomatoes and enjoy their real good flavor. Children particularly enjoy the outing and get to see that peas come in pods, or that milk comes from a cow.
—*Joe Carcione 1986*

Pick-it-yourself operations in the Bay Area are recommended by columnist and television and radio personality "The Green-Grocer" Joe Carcione. Small growers are virtually the only ones staying in business and produce over one hundred food crops. Prime soils that have not been paved over are found in eastern Contra Costa County, the coastside of San Mateo County, southern Santa Clara County, Solano County, and parts of Napa and Sonoma counties. Seen here is a family's annual outing to pick tomatoes and other produce on a Sonoma County farm.

When the Big One comes, predictable things will happen. People will be thrown across flexible steel frame structures and crushed by moving office furniture. Unreinforced brick buildings and some high rises are likely to collapse on their own, while others that have been built flush to one another will likely demolish each other as they begin oscillating at different frequencies. Tons of glass and facing veneers will rain into the streets which may themselves subside.

What happens next is even scarier. In those streets will be not only people, but thousands of automobiles, each with a gas tank. Crushed, there will be free gasoline all over downtown. Then there will be a fire, as in 1906. But unlike 1906, there will be no way for people to get out through blocked streets. Nor will it be possible for the Fire Department to get in, even if they were capable of fighting simultaneous fires in high rises.
—*San Franciscans for Reasonable Growth 1984*

Downtown San Francisco's weekday population is four hundred thousand, and thousands will die if a major earthquake along the San Andreas fault strikes at rush hour. According to the Federal Emergency Management Agency, area-wide up to thirty thousand people would be killed. Violent movement along the Hayward fault in the East Bay would cause slightly fewer fatalities. Aside from damage caused by building failure, bayside lands could be inundated, bridges collapse, and dams break. Seen opposite is a 1986 view of the intersection of Front Street with Market Street, the main thoroughfare of downtown San Francisco.

The Crossroads Community, also known as "The Farm," located under the Highway 101–Army Street interchange in San Francisco, was founded by conceptual artist Bonnie Sherk with Jack Wickert in 1974 to bring city and country living together for the benefit of the urban community. A cultural center with many unwitting participants speeding above at fifty miles an hour, it is popular with school groups and has a theater, art gallery, and a day-care program (pictured).

On the interchange outside our window there are thirty-six points of conflict. Precisely thirty-six places where people can crash into each other. It's always close. There's one wall they smack into all the time. It's not for the people; the wall shouldn't be there at all.

By growing things here, we're making the air a lot better. That's a real practical application of accepting trees and other plants as part of our lives. There are a lot of human life-giving activities here. There are a lot of animals here, too: chickens, rabbits, hundreds of ladybugs, spiders, worms, birds, cats, a dog. The farm is also our home, and when people come we share a living room and a kitchen together. —*Jack Wickert and Bonnie Sherk 1978*

The Salt-Marsh Harvest Mouse survives or dies out in rhythm with local, food-based, economy. Now, with 80% of the original Bay Area Marsh filled for residential and industrial development, the Salt-Marsh Harvest Mouse is an endangered species. And, in rhythm with its population, 90% of the Bay's shellfish area has disappeared. (Shellfish have more protein than beef.) The tiny, salt-marsh mouse is rich brown or blackish cinnamon with rust-colored belly. It evolved only in the marshes of the Bay and Delta. Known for its non-aggressive lifestyle, this rodent lives in song sparrow nests to escape the tides and enters a state of suspended animation whenever it's chilly. The Salt-Marsh [Harvest Mouse] is our Animal Totem. Restoring its home, protecting its gardens from dredging and filling means restoring our nearby food sources and making paradise the place where you live. — *Frisco Bay Mussel Group 1978*

Until the 1960s there were few legal restraints on filling San Francisco Bay, of which at least a quarter had already been filled since the Gold Rush for new farmland, housing, garbage disposal sites, airports, and other urban developments. Of the remainder, a quarter was privately owned and in imminent danger of being filled. Public pressure for the bay's protection led to the formation of the Bay Conservation and Development Commission in 1965, a state-mandated agency that tightly regulates filling and promotes recreational use of the bay, its shore, and marshlands. Marshland is not only the beginning of many food chains but also removes pollutants from the air and water and, as part of the water surface, moderates summer and winter climates. Of the salt-marsh harvest mouse, little is known, but the endangered species has become the environmentalists' trump card in battles over bayshore development.

The commonest trees, bugs, and breezes tell stories that apply everywhere; there are worlds beneath each rock. By knowing our neighborhood, we begin to understand the universe. — *Yosemite National Institutes 1985*

The ecological view of the world as a natural system of checks and balances holds that all life forms—including mankind—are interdependent. In the 1930s and 1940s this scientific view began to replace the spiritual aura accorded nature by preservationists. By the 1960s ecology was popularized and widely taught in schools, as it is today.

Where nature is neglected, it may become a formidable opponent, and most communities bear the scars of such past mistakes in the form of housing tracts that are periodically flooded; roads, sewers, or waterlines that are cut or endangered by landslides; or ponds of effluent that seep from poorly sited septic-tank drainfields. —*Robert D. Brown, Jr., and William K. Kockelman 1983*

In the Bay Area every resident is risking being caught in the natural catastrophe of a violent earthquake, but people living or working in floodplains and on steep hillsides live in double jeopardy. Civil engineers who calculate flood hazards base precautionary measures on the theoretical once-in-hundred-years flood. However nature is no slave to probabilities, and in any case communities are often reluctant to adopt drastic measures. Seen in the top photograph is Bolinas Road in Fairfax, Marin County, 1982. Below are flooded fields near Sonoma Creek, 1986.

Back-to-back storms last week pumped enough fresh rain into the Delta/Bay waterways to set the striper migration in full gear. In San Francisco Bay, the bass are taking off, heading through San Pablo and Suisun Bays. . . . High and outgoing tides seem to have set off the best fishing. . . . As winter approaches, some one million stripers will be heading up to the Delta. —*Tom Stienstra 1984*

The striped bass is San Francisco Bay's major sport fish, its population monitored by the California Department of Fish and Game. Introduced at Martinez in 1879, the striped bass flourished in its new home, apparently occupying an ecological niche that had not been taken in the relatively young (ten-thousand-year-old) Pacific estuarine system. In the 1950s a million fish a year were caught. Since then the bay population has fluctuated widely, responding to rain and snow levels, how much fresh water (taking young fish with it) is diverted from the Sacramento River, and water pollution. Between 1975 and 1985 the juvenile population dropped by ninety percent and has shown little improvement since. The striped bass, shown here being measured by a warden at Martinez, has been compared to the miner's canary as an indicator of the bay's fate. Other popular sport fish are sturgeon, salmon, steelhead trout, and shad, the last also introduced in the 1870s to the Sacramento River system.

For over 200 years the open land of the Bay Area has served the people who live here. It has been garden and ranch, woodlot and quarry, watershed and game preserve. Within it we have built a major metropolis that now requires more in resources than our nine counties alone can provide. But the richness close to home is still a major support for life in the Bay Area, and one of the things that makes Bay Area living good.

Over the years we have learned to value our remaining natural landscape. We have protected key elements: our magnificent parks, our watershed, our habitat reserves, our open Bay and tidelands.

But this progress has not kept pace with change. The metropolis once contained in a few compact centers now has outposts, extensions, and influences in every corner of the Bay Area. What was a collection of separate cities and towns has become a single urban organism, a supercity. There is grandeur in this but danger also—the city threatens to overwhelm the countryside, [and with it, the source of our richness].
—*People for Open Space 1980*

Almost four million acres of the Bay Area's diverse landscape is open land, of which nearly a quarter is protected as public watershed and parkland. Much ranch and crop land is under increasing pressure from urban development because of high land values, expensive support services, and intolerant suburban neighbors. Contra Costa County—where this photograph of a roundup was taken—has lost one hundred thousand acres of pasture to roads and urban and suburban development since 1940; less than two hundred thousand remain. The story is nearly as dramatic for the Bay Area as a whole. Preservation of agricultural land was the aim of California's Williamson Act of 1965, which gives a tax break to farmers who promise not to develop their land; imposition of a minimum parcel size in designated farming areas has the same purpose. In another scheme, private land trusts buy guarantees from farmers not to develop land for residential or commercial use. According to People for Open Space, an area-wide organization dedicated to preserving the greenbelt around urban areas, a growing population can be accommodated within existing municipalities for at least the next two decades.

No city in California possesses a more valuable scenic asset than the shoreline of San Francisco—in fact, few cities anywhere rejoice in such a priceless natural resource. The San Francisco shore is an incomparably crisp, neat, well-drawn municipal boundary line, shimmering, blue-gray fringe, thirty-five miles long, enclosing the city on three sides, dimpled with coves and inlets, basins and ship canals. More important, it is an exhilarating influence upon the people of the city, drawing their vision outward, opening their physical and mental horizons and infusing them with a sense of natural grandeur and a spirit of adventure. —*Richard Reinhardt 1971*

Eleven miles of ocean bluffs, beaches, and piers of San Francisco's western shoreline are protected from private development by the Golden Gate National Recreation Area. Seen here from near Land's End are Phelan and Baker beaches and, to the left, the forested Presidio, home of the Sixth Army. Eastward from Fisherman's Wharf and southward along the San Francisco bay-shore, only a few public promenades break the succession of docks and shipyards served by rail lines tracing the Embarcadero. The eastern shore is best seen from Yerba Buena Island and the city's hills: Telegraph, Potrero, and Bernal Heights. San Francisco's shore is a magnificent asset in itself, but it has also hemmed in urban energy to create a concentrated city whose fame is quite disproportionate to its size and population.

This loveliest of American cities is in mortal danger of total disappearance. There is the remorseless brutalization of the uniquely delicate skyline, and the obliteration of everyone's view. All that clean air is filling up with Big Black Specks from pollution, and the famous clarity of the light is fading away forever. . . . San Francisco is the last civilized outpost in the U.S.A., and damn well worth conserving, *now*, before hell strikes it. —*Holiday magazine 1970*

The first generation of San Francisco's highrises grew in the 1920s, and this was the profile the nation knew until the early 1960s. The upper photograph, opposite, was taken in the 1950s. The Crown Zellerbach Building of 1959 and the Golden Gateway townhouses (seen at the foot of the Transamerica pyramid) of the early 1960s initiated a downtown building boom fired by plans for BART, a new rapid transit system in operation from 1974. The fifty-two-story Bank of America Building of 1970–71 is prominent in the middle photograph. The lower view of the downtown skyline was taken in 1986. Restrictions on construction, imposed under public pressure, have been honored more in their circumvention than in their observation. In 1907 building heights were restricted to 100 feet except along Market Street. In 1939, 105 feet was the limit in Pacific Heights, 290 feet on Telegraph Hill. Bulk restrictions were established in 1960 and amended in 1966 and 1968. Apparently only economics will decide whether construction will continue until towers stand shoulder to shoulder from Telegraph hill south to Sixteenth Street.

1950s

1970

1986

The ancient trees stand to support Heaven
Lest Heaven should fall.
Its falling is impossible,
Yet they have stood there, upholding the clouds—
how many years?
In the thousands of centuries before my knowledge
Fairies and spirits lived above the clouds.
I come now from the Eastern land to travel silently;
I neither met immortals nor was able to see the sky.
Suddenly a shaft of sunshine shoots through the trees,
Bright yellow and young green divide the beauty.
These giants of trees reveal my insignificance.
From some hidden corner, deep in the hills
a brook flows on—

Its intermittent murmurs make the peace profounder.
Swaying creepers, hanging from the cliff,
disturb the clear mist.
Mist spirals up to circle the tree tops;
Invisibly a few birds perch in the foliage:
Their birds' talk is audible then quiet,
At one time they chatter, at another they are silent.
For the moment I close my mind to dusty,
earthly affairs,
And receive the murmurs that come down from
ages long past.
How can I hope for a second living span?
Lingering on I hum leisurely for my enjoyment.

—*Chiang Yee 1960s*

Few are the redwood groves that survived the pioneer's axe. Among them are Marin's Steep Ravine (pictured opposite) and neighboring Muir Woods National Monument, where author Chiang Yee found echoes of China's mountain hermitages.

A Miwok-Pomo Indian child, a proud descendant of the original inhabitants of the Bay Area, dances nimbly at Kule Loklo (Miwok for "bear valley") in Point Reyes National Seashore as part of a demonstration of traditional arts. Dancing was essential to maintain a harmonious relationship with the earth and was also performed as a ritual cure for sickness and at ceremonies honoring the dead. Today, on private occasions, dancing still fulfills some of these functions for the small numbers of Native Americans living in Marin and Sonoma counties. In the East Bay, a group of native people descended from Costanoans (as they were named by the Spaniards) in 1971 reformed as the Ohlone Indian Tribe.

If the whites and all minorities except the Indians were suddenly to disappear and the erstwhile native people were to possess the state once again, how would they fare? Acorn mush might become once more a standard food; the salmon would again run the rivers (in ever larger numbers as the great Corps of Engineers and Bureau of Reclamation river dams burst from lack of maintenance); the deer would multiply enormously without predators such as the Grizzly Bear and the mountain lion; and there would be amply bearing orchards of introduced fruit ready for the picking. All of this would require a period of relearning for the Indians, not only to forget the habits and devices of "civilization" but also to master once more the ancient knowledge, skills and artifacts of the ancestral people, which have, in little more than a century, been quite lost or forgotten. If the Indians were regranted their patrimony, they might make out rather well. —*Robert F. Heizer and Albert B. Elsasser 1980*

Golden Gate National Recreation Area finds its meaning in [the] sequence of urban growth. The park protects the land as it once was and the history it represents; now, more than ever before, people need this diminishing source of relaxation and beauty.

The past gives the park its richness. Thousands of years ago, geologic forces created the terrain; towering coastal redwoods, as well as second growth forests and grasslands provide habitats for a variety of wildlife. Human history—archeological sites, old sailing ships, ranch houses, and military fortifications—demonstrates this land's importance to the region's early livelihood and protection. —*Golden Gate National Recreation Area 1985*

Established in 1972, the Golden Gate National Recreation Area incorporates most of the northern shoreline of San Francisco, Alcatraz Island, thousands of acres of open country across the Golden Gate Bridge in Marin County, and Sweeney Ridge in San Mateo County. Marin's annual Dipsea Race (lower photograph), with an eighty-year history, traverses three park systems on its treacherous 7.1-mile route from Mill Valley to Stinson Beach. In the East Bay, a slightly smaller acreage of wooded parkland runs the length of the hills between El Cerrito and Castro Valley. Many of the parks in the Bay Area consist of uplands that were impracticable for housing in the nineteenth century and were therefore reserved for watershed or military use. Preserved by these fortuitous circumstances, lands that later became available for development were pressed into use as public parks and are now a vital part of urban life in the Bay Area.

California can do whatever it wants. It can use its mountains to fill in San Francisco Bay and the ocean above the continental shelf and there build more suburbs and parking lots. It can exterminate any and all species of birds, mammals, and plants. Or it can restrict or ban the car, the bulldozer, the subdivider, and the speculator. It can save or reconstitute much of its agriculture, as it can much of its shore line and mountain back country. Salvation is as possible as destruction.
—*Richard Lillard 1968*

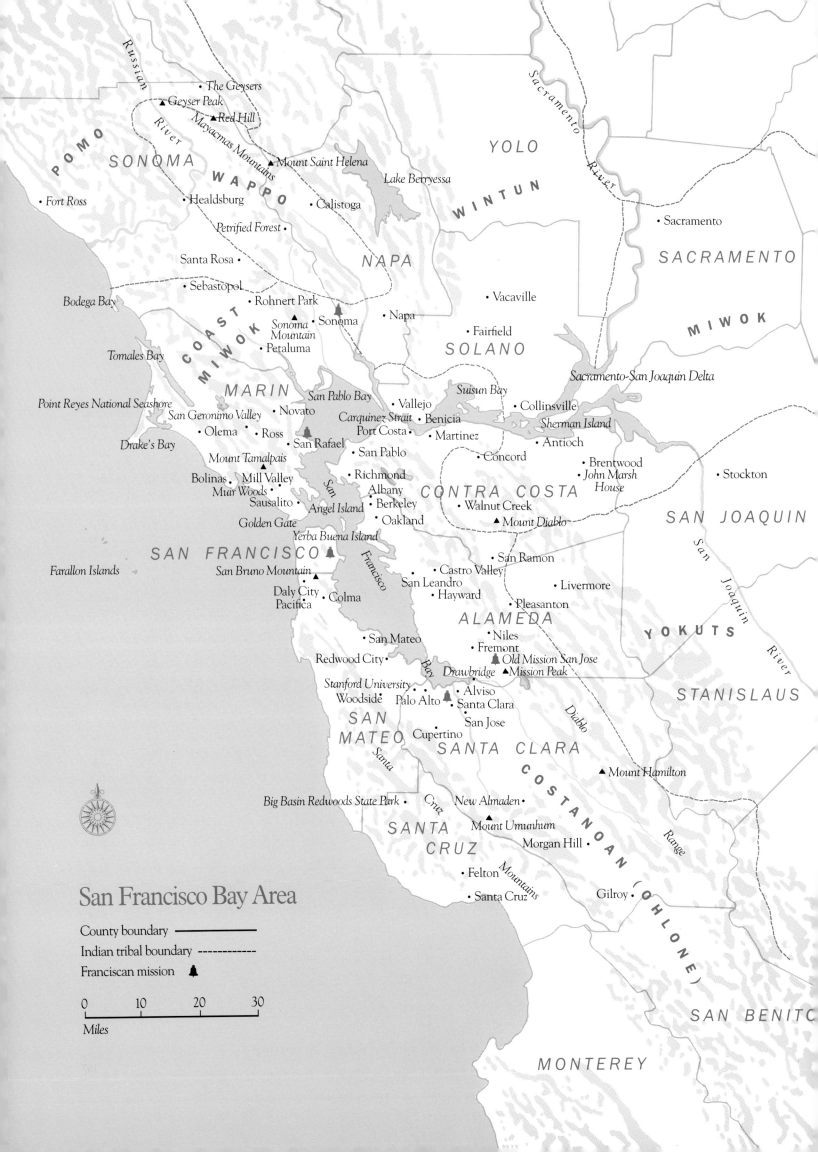

Russian River

• The Geysers
▲ Geyser Peak
▲ Red Hill
Mayacmas Mountains
▲ Mount Saint Helena

POMO

SONOMA

WAPPO

NAPA

• Fort Ross

• Healdsburg

• Calistoga

Petrified Forest •

Lake Berryessa

Santa Rosa •

Bodega Bay

• Sebastopol

• Rohnert Park

COAST

• Sonoma
▲ Sonoma
  Mountain
• Petaluma

• Napa

YOLO

Sacramento River

WINTUN

• Sacramento

SACRAMENTO

• Vacaville

• Fairfield

SOLANO

MIWOK

Tomales Bay

MIWOK

Point Reyes National Seashore

MARIN

San Pablo Bay

Sacramento-San Joaquin Delta

San Geronimo Valley

• Novato

Suisun Bay

• Vallejo

• Collinsville

Sherman Island

• Olema • Ross

Carquinez Strait • Benicia

Drake's Bay

• San Rafael

Port Costa •

• Martinez

• Antioch

Mount Tamalpais

• San Pablo

• Concord

• Brentwood
• John Marsh
  House

• Stockton

Bolinas • • Mill Valley

• Richmond

Muir Woods

Albany

CONTRA COSTA

Sausalito •

• Berkeley

• Walnut Creek

SAN JOAQUIN

Angel Island

• Oakland

▲ Mount Diablo

Golden Gate

Yerba Buena Island

San

SAN FRANCISCO

Francisco

• San Ramon

San Joaquin River

Farallon Islands

San Bruno Mountain

• Castro Valley

Daly City

San Leandro

• Livermore

Pacifica

• Colma

• Hayward

• Pleasanton

ALAMEDA

YOKUTS

• San Mateo

• Niles

Redwood City •

• Fremont

Bay

Drawbridge

Old Mission San Jose
▲ Mission Peak

STANISLAUS

Stanford University

• Alviso

Woodside •

Palo Alto

• Santa Clara

SAN

Cupertino

• San Jose

Diablo

MATEO

SANTA CLARA

Santa

COSTANOAN (OHLONE)

▲ Mount Hamilton

Big Basin Redwoods State Park •

Cruz

• New Almaden •

SANTA

▲ Mount Umunhum

Range

CRUZ

• Morgan Hill

• Felton

Mountains

• Santa Cruz

• Gilroy

San Francisco Bay Area

County boundary ———
Indian tribal boundary - - - - -
Franciscan mission ▲

0   10   20   30
Miles

SAN BENITO

MONTEREY

Sources and Locations

Sources of historical quotations and illustrations are herein listed by text page number. In addition to alterations specifically noted, in some cases small changes have been made in the interest of readability. Information concerning locations photographed is also included when additional to specifics given in the photo captions.

The World of Coyote-man

12 Clinton Hart Merriam, *Dawn of the World* (Glendale: Arthur H. Clark, 1910), 15. *Illustration:* from Adelbert Chamisso, *A Sojourn at San Francisco Bay* (San Francisco: Book Club of California, 1936), 12.

13 Pomo carrying basket, Treganza Museum of Anthropology, San Francisco State U.

15 Coast Miwok tale, as related in Merriam, 203. Reprinted by permission. *Photograph:* top of Sonoma Mountain (elev. 2463 ft.) 7 mi. east of Cotati, Sonoma County. Private land.

16 Coast Miwok tale, as related in Merriam, 159. Reprinted by permission. *Photograph:* Mount Tamalpais (elev. 2571 ft.) from north with coast live oak, Mount Tamalpais State Park, west of Mill Valley, Marin County.

18 Coast Miwok tale, as related in Merriam, 135. Reprinted by permission. *Photographs:* valley oak, Marin County; prairie falcon, San Francisco Zoo; coyote, Wildlife Associates, Pacifica, San Mateo County.

19 Francis Fletcher, *The World Encompassed by Sir Francis Drake* (London: Bourne, 1628), 79.

20 Alexander Forbes, *California* (London: Smith, Elder, 1839), 120. *Photographs:* obsidian arrowpoints from Marin County, Treganza Museum, San Francisco State University; Pomo basket, Lowie Museum of Anthropology, UC Berkeley.

21 Juan Bautista de Anza, as quoted in Herbert E. Bolton, *Anza's California Expeditions* (Berkeley: University of California Press, 1930), vol. 3, 146. Reprinted by permission.

Jean François de Galaup, Comte de La Pérouse, as quoted in Forbes, 120.

22 Fathers Narciso Durán and Buenaventura Fortuny, as quoted in Francis F. McCarthy, *The History of Mission San Jose* (Fresno: Academy Library Guild, 1958), 272.

Pedro Fages, *A Historical, Political, and Natural Description of California,* trans. Herbert Ingram Priestley (Berkeley: University of California Press, 1937), 76. Reprinted by permission.

23 *Photograph:* mortar rock, San Diego Rd. and Indian Rock Ave., Berkeley.

24 Peter Corney, *Voyages in the Northern Pacific* (Honolulu: Thrum, 1896), 33–34.

Coast Miwok tale, as related in Merriam, 217. Reprinted by permission.

This Kingdome

26 *Illustration:* from Frank Soulé, John H. Gihon, and James Nisbet, *Annals of San Francisco* (New York: Appleton, 1855), 29.

29 Fletcher, 79, 80. *Photograph:* Inverness Ridge and Olema Valley, Point Reyes National Seashore, Marin County.

30-31 Father Juan Crespí, as quoted in George Butler Griffin, "Documents from the Sutro Collection," in *Publication of Historical Society of Southern California* (Los Angeles), vol. 1, part 1 (1891), 210.

32 Father Juan Crespí, as quoted in Herbert E. Bolton, *Fray Juan Crespí, Missionary Explorer on the Pacific Coast, 1769–1774* (Berkeley: University of California Press, 1927), 290. Reprinted by permission.

33 Father Francisco Palóu, *Historical Memoirs of New California,* trans. Herbert E. Bolton (Berkeley: University of California Press, 1926), vol. 3, 263. Reprinted by permission.

34 Father Juan Crespí, as quoted in Palóu, vol. 2, 220. Reprinted by permission. *Photograph:* holly-leaf cherry, Botanical Garden, University of California, Berkeley, Alameda County.

Jean François de Galaup, Comte de La Pérouse, *A Voyage of La Pérouse Round the World* (London: 1798), vol. 1, 201.

35 Father Juan Crespí, as quoted in Bolton, *Fray Juan Crespí,* 45. Reprinted by permission.

36 José Cañizares, as quoted in John Galvin, *The First Spanish Entry into San Francisco Bay, 1775* (San Francisco: Howell, 1971), 96.

37 Father Pedro Font, as quoted in Bolton, *Anza's California Expeditions,* vol. 4, 262. Reprinted by permission. *Photograph:* redwood, Alma St. and Palo Alto Ave., Palo Alto, Santa Clara Co.

Palóu, vol. 4, 124. Reprinted by permission.

38 Mariano Guadalupe Vallejo, as quoted in Ray W. Taylor, *Hetch Hetchy* (San Francisco: Orozco, 1926), 10. *Photograph:* El Polín spring with seep-spring or common monkeyflower *(Mimulus guttatus),* south end of McArthur Ave., San Francisco Presidio.

Nikolai Aleksandrovich Khvostov, as quoted in Richard A. Pierce, *Rezanov Reconnoiters California, 1806* (San Francisco: Book Club of California, 1972), 50. Reprinted by permission.

I Am a Christian Indian

40 *Illustration:* from Eugène Duflot de Mofras, *Exploration du territoire de l'Oregon, des Californies* (Paris: Société Geographie, 1844), 203.

42 Father Vicente Santa María, as quoted in Galvin, 49.

43 *Photograph:* baptismal font (c. 1830) Old Mission San Jose, Fremont, Alameda County. Overprinted are entries by Father José María de Jesús González Rubio in "Libro de bautismos," vol 2., of Mission San Jose. Manuscript in possession of Archdiocese of San Francisco Archives. Reproduced by permission.

44 Otto von Kotzebue, *Voyage of Discovery in the South Sea and to Behring's Straits* (London: Phillips, 1821), 76. *Photograph:* Mission Dolores, Dolores and Sixteenth streets, San Francisco.

45 Louis Choris, *Voyage pittoresque autour du monde* (Paris: Didiot, 1822), 2–3. Excerpt trans. Charles Kennard.

46 Franciscan missionary, as quoted in Arthur Quinn, *Broken Shore: The Marin Peninsula* (Salt Lake City: Peregrine Smith: 1981), 58. *Photograph:* roof timbers, Old Mission San Jose, Fremont, Alameda County.

Georg Heinrich von Langsdorff, *Bemerkungen auf einer Reise um die Welt* (Frankfurt am Mein: Wilmans, 1812), vol. 2, 167. Excerpt trans. Eva Seligman Kennard. *Photograph:* pears from a tree grafted from the original Mission San Rafael trees, Marin Art and Garden Center, Sir Francis Drake Blvd., Ross, Marin County.

47 Frederick W. Beechey, *Narrative of a Voyage to the Pacific and Beering's Strait* (London: Colburn and Bentley, 1831), vol. 2, 79. *Photograph:* mountain lion, Wildlife Associates, Pacifica, San Mateo Co.

48 Auguste Bernard Duhaut-Cilly, "Duhaut-Cilly's Account of California in the Years 1827–28," trans. Charles F. Carter, *California Historical Society Quarterly* 8:3 (September 1929), 240. Reprinted by permission. *Photograph:* freshwater marsh, Coyote Hills Regional Park, Fremont, Alameda County.

49 Eugène Duflot de Mofras, *Travels on the Pacific Coast*, trans. Marguerite E. Wilbur (Santa Ana: Fine Arts, 1937), 237. *Photograph:* bell, Mission San Rafael, Fifth and A streets, San Rafael, Marin County.

Edward Vischer, "Edward Vischer's First Visit to California," trans. Erwin G. Gudde, *California Historical Society Quarterly* 19:3 (September 1940), 198. Reprinted by permission.

50 María Copa Frías, as quoted in "Coast Miwok Field Notes 1931–1932, Marin Subgroup," note 1:14b. Manuscript by Isabel T. Kelly, in possession of Robert V. Kemper, Isabel T. Kelly Ethnographic Archive, Department of Anthropology, Southern Methodist University, Dallas, Texas. Printed by permission. *Photograph:* northern Pacific rattlesnake, Sutter County.

51 Indian of Mission Dolores, as quoted in Edward D. Castillo, "The Impact of Euro-American Exploration and Settlement," *Handbook of North American Indians*, ed. Robert Heizer (Washington: Smithsonian, 1978), vol. 8, 105. Quotation rearranged in verse form. *Photograph:* crucifix, Mission Dolores Museum.

La Yerba Buena

52 *Illustration:* from Soulé et al., 170. *Photograph:* Mexican spur, Lowie Museum of Anthropology, University of California, Berkeley.

54 *Photograph:* Peralta Adobe, 184 Saint John St., San Jose, Santa Clara County. Overprinted is letter from Luís María Peralta to Spanish governor of California Pablo Vicente Solá, dated June 20, 1820. Manuscript as p 5, Complete Expediente 186, California Private Land Claims (Division E), Records of the Bureau of Land Management (Record Group 49), National Archives and Records Administration, Washington, D.C.

55 Luís Peralta, as quoted in Frances L. Fox, *Luís María Peralta and His Adobe* (San Jose: Smith-McKay, 1975), 37.

José Ramón Estrada, letter in Spanish reproduced in Phyllis Filiberti Butler, *The Valley of Santa Clara* (Novato: Presidio, 1975), 71. Excerpt trans. Charles Kennard. *Photograph:* Peña Adobe (Santa Clara Women's Club), 3260 The Alameda, Santa Clara, Santa Clara County.

56-57 William Brewer, *Up and Down California in 1860–1864* (Berkeley and Los Angeles: University of California Press, 1966), 257. Reprinted by permission. *Map: diseño* of Rancho Cañada de Herrera, granted to Domingo Sais. Land case map B139 (65ND), courtesy The Bancroft Library, University of California, Berkeley.

58 Edwin Bryant, *What I Saw in California* (Palo Alto: Osborne, 1967), 338. *Photograph:* Petaluma Adobe State Historic Park, Casa Grande and Adobe roads, east of Petaluma, Sonoma County.

59 George Simpson, *Narrative of a Voyage to California* (San Francisco: Russell, 1930), 67. *Photograph:* wall of Camilo Ynitia's adobe, Olompali State Historic Park (undeveloped), west of Hwy. 101, 2.8 mi. north of Atherton Ave., Novato, Marin Co.

Bryant, 305. *Photograph:* longhorn cattle, near Alamo, Contra Costa Co.

60 *Photograph:* Vallejo (or Mission) Adobe, on grounds of Mission Adobe Nursery, 36501 Niles Blvd., Niles, Alameda County.

61 Guadalupe de Jesús Vallejo, "Ranch and Mission Days in Alta California," *Century* 19 (December 1890), 185.

José de Jesús Vallejo, as quoted in *California Pastoral*, The Works of Hubert Howe Bancroft, vol. 34 (San Francisco: The History Co., 1888), 330.

62 Lansford Hastings, *Emigrant's Guide to Oregon and California* (Cincinnati: Conclin, 1845), 87.

John Charles Frémont, *Geographical Memoir Upon Upper California* (Washington: Wendell and Van Benthuysen, 1848), 33.

63 Bayard Taylor, *El Dorado* (New York: Knopf, 1949), 50–51.

64-65 *Photograph:* Old Mill Park, Throckmorton Ave., Mill Valley, Marin County.

66 Frank Marryat, *Mountains and Molehills* (New York: Harper, 1855), 95–96 (describing William March's mill near Healdsburg).

Alfred Robinson, *Life in California* (Oakland: Biobooks, 1947), 136.

67 John Charles Frémont, *Exploring Expedition to the Rocky Mountains, Oregon and Northern California* (Washington: Gales and Seaton, 1845), 358.

Hastings, 99. *Photograph:* snow geese, December 1983, Sacramento National Wildlife Refuge.

68 Mofras, *Travels on the Pacific Coast*, 7. *Photographs:* Fort Ross State Historic Park, Hwy. 1, Sonoma County.

70 Hastings, 110. *Photograph:* Hastings Adobe, ½ mi. east of Collinsville, south Solano County. Private land.

71 Joseph Warren Revere, *Naval Duty in California* (Oakland: Biobooks, 1947), 63. *Photographs:* Sonoma Barracks, Sonoma State Historic Park, Sonoma County; Bear Flag, from a photographic copy of the original destroyed in 1906.

Heavy to Get, Light to Hold

72 *Illustration:* from Marryat, 48. *Photograph:* ship's compass, National Maritime Museum, San Francisco.

74 Anonymous poem, quoted in Catherine C. Phillips, *Portsmouth Plaza, the Cradle of San Francisco* (San Francisco: Nash, 1932), 146. *Photograph:* gold leaf on matrix, c. 4" high, C.A.S. #1081, California Academy of Sciences, San Francisco.

75 Christopher Allyn, as quoted in the *Daily Chronicle* (New London, Conn.), September 15, 1848. Excerpt in display at the National Maritime Museum, San Francisco. *Photograph:* ship's knee, #7971 acc. 107, 57″ × 37″ × 10″, National Maritime Museum, San Francisco.

Evening Picayune (San Francisco), September 30, 1850, as quoted in Kenneth M. Johnson, *San Francisco As It Is* (Georgetown: Talisman, 1964), 57. *Photograph:* artifacts, Lowie Museum of Anthropology, UC Berkeley.

76 Etienne Derbec, *A French Journalist in the California Gold Rush*, ed. A. P. Nasatir (Georgetown: Talisman, 1964), 170. Reprinted by permission. *Photograph:* Vásquez House, Sonoma League for Historic Preservation, El Paseo, Spain and First streets, Sonoma, Sonoma County.

Walter Colton, as quoted in Phillips, 423. *Photograph:* 31 Alta St., San Francisco.

77 Frank Soulé et al., 414. *Photograph:* Belli Building, 722 Montgomery St., San Francisco; Genella Building, 728 Montgomery St.

William Tecumseh Sherman, as quoted in Dwight L. Clarke, *William Tecumseh Sherman: Gold Rush Banker* (San Francisco: California Historical Society, 1969), 40. *Photograph:* (former) Bank of Lucas, Turner and Co., 800 Montgomery St., San Francisco.

78 J. G. Barnard, as quoted in J. G. Motheral, *Fort Point, Gibraltar of the Pacific* (San Francisco: Fort Point Museum Assoc., 1971), 6. *Photographs:* Fort Point National Historic Site, San Francisco.

79 *Placer Times and Transcript* (San Francisco), December 30, 1852, as quoted in *Benicia Capitol State Historic Park* (pamphlet) (California Department of Parks and Recreation, 1985). *Photograph:* Benicia Capitol State Historic Park, First and G streets, Benicia, Solano County.

Legal contract, Book A, Deeds, 13–14, Marin County Recorder's Office. *Photograph:* Olema Lime Kilns, 5 mi. south of Olema, near Hwy. marker 22.22, by creek on west side of Hwy. 1, Marin County.

80 *Daily Evening Bulletin* (San Francisco), July 19, 1856, 1. *Photograph:* John Marsh House State Historic Park (closed), on Marsh Creek Rd. 4 mi. southwest of Brentwood, Contra Costa County.

Marryat, 311.

81 Marryat, 127. *Photograph:* bobcat, Wildlife Associates, Pacifica, San Mateo County.

John W. Audubon, *Audubon's Western Journal: 1849–1850* (Cleveland: Clark, 1906), 185.

82 Bayard Taylor, *New Pictures from California* (Oakland: Biobooks, 1951), 14.

Brewer, 156 (describing the Santa Cruz Mountains). Reprinted by permission.

83 *Photograph:* view from Mount Diablo (elev. 3849 ft.) to southwest in January, Mount Diablo State Park, east of Walnut Creek, Contra Costa County.

84 Brewer, 295. Reprinted by permission. *Photographs*: Malakoff Diggins State Park, North Bloomfield, Nevada County; Sacramento River, Horseshoe Bend from Sherman Island, Solano and Sacramento counties.

85 Brewer, 174. Reprinted by permission. *Photograph*: view to northeast from Mission Peak Regional Preserve. Trail to peak from Ohlone College, Mission Blvd., Fremont, Alameda Co.

Come One! Come All!

86 Chapter opening quotation from *Oakland Enquirer*, January 1888, 4. *Illustration*: from Lucius Beebe and Charles Clegg, *San Francisco's Golden Era* (Berkeley: Howell-North, 1960), 236.

87 John Muir letter to his sister Sarah, c. 1871–75, as quoted in Linnie M. Wolfe, *Son of the Wilderness* (New York: Knopf, 1945), 165.

88 Noah Brooks, as quoted in *San Francisco Real Estate Circular*, October 1883, 1. *Photograph*: Ohlhoff House (1891), 601 Steiner St., San Francisco.

89 Justin McCarthy (1830–1912), *Lady Judith, a Tale of Two Continents* (New York: Sheldon: 1871), as quoted in the *San Francisco Chronicle*, January 1, 1891, 26. Quotation rearranged in verse form. *Photograph*: Mount Olympus (elev. 570 ft.), Monument Way, view north from Twin Peaks, San Francisco.

90 Guillermo Prieto, *San Francisco in the Seventies*, trans. Edwin S. Morby (San Francisco: Nash, 1938), 4 (describing the Gailhard Hotel).

Eugene Bandel, *Frontier Life in the Army 1854–1861* (Glendale: Arthur H. Clarke, 1932), 303. Reprinted by permission.

91 Prieto, 6–7. *Photograph*: Hotaling Buildings, 445, 451, 463–473 Jackson St., San Francisco.

92 *Photograph*: Octagon House, 2645 Gough St., San Francisco. Overprinted is letter from William C. McElroy: "To Future Ageses" (sic). Courtesy of National Society of Colonial Dames in California, San Francisco.

93 Orson Fowler, *The Octagon House, A Home for All* (New York: Dover, 1973), 82.

San Francisco Chronicle, © San Francisco Chronicle, March 28, 1907. Reprinted by permission.

94 Josiah Royce, *California* (New York: Knopf, 1948), 171.

95 Frederick Law Olmsted, as quoted in *San Francisco Municipal Reports 1865–1866*, 397.

96 Rudyard Kipling, *American Notes* (Boston: Brown, 1899), 19. *Photographs*: cable cars, Cable Car Museum, 1201 Mason St., San Francisco.

97 William H. Bishop, "San Francisco," *Harpers New Monthly Magazine* (New York), vol. 66 (May 1883), 831. *Photograph*: Kong Chow Association memorial, visible to north from Legion of Honor Dr., Lincoln Park, San Francisco.

W. W. Elliott, *Oakland and Surroundings* (Oakland: Elliott, c. 1885), 60.

98 Benjamin Taylor, *Between the Gates* (Chicago: Griggs, 1878), 68. *Photograph*: Pardee House, Pardee House Foundation, 672 Eleventh St., Oakland, Alameda County.

Charles H. Shinn, *Pacific Rural Handbook*, (San Francisco: Dewey, 1879), 100.

99 *Photograph*: James Shinn House (1876), Shinn Historical Park, 1251 Peralta Ave. at Sidney Dr., Fremont, Alameda County.

100 *California, Home for the Emigrant* (San Francisco: California Immigrant Union, 1878), 2. *Photograph*: farmhouse and valley, view west from Mission Peak Regional Pre-serve. Trail to peak from Ohlone College, Mission Blvd., Fremont, Alameda County.

101 *San Francisco Daily Morning Call*, June 14, 1895, 9. *Photograph*: Port Costa, with church built in the 1890s, view from southwest to Carquinez Strait and Benicia, Contra Costa and Solano counties.

Titus Fey Cronise, *The Natural Wealth of California* (San Francisco: H. H. Bancroft, 1868), 149.

102 George H. Fitch, "The Santa Clara Valley," in *West of the Rocky Mountains*, ed. John Muir (Philadelphia: Running Press, 1976), 290.

103 Agoston Haraszthy, *Grape Culture and Wines and Wine Making* (New York: Harper, 1862), 111.

104 S. A. Downer, as quoted in J. M. Hutchings, *Scenes of Wonder and Curiosity* (San Francisco: Roman, 1870), 193.

Cronise, 152–153.

105 *Photographs*: salt ponds, view west from Coyote Hills Regional Park, Fremont, Alameda County; salt pile, Port of Redwood City, San Mateo County.

106 Charles Nordhoff, *Northern California, Oregon and the Sandwich Islands* (New York: Harper, 1874), 178.

107 *California, Home for the Emigrant*, 22.

San Mateo County Gazette (Redwood City), April 16, 1859, as quoted in "Woodside and Searsville in 1859," *La Peninsula* 6:5 (May 1952), 6.

108-109 *Photograph*: Woodside Store, County Parks and Recreation Dept., King's Mountain and Tripp roads, Woodside, San Mateo County.

110 T. J. Butts, as quoted in W. L. Gaston, *Golden Jubilee History of the First Baptist Church* (Santa Rosa: Re-publican, 1902), 33. *Photograph*: Church of One Tree, Ripley Believe It or Not Museum, north side of Juilliard Park, Santa Rosa, Sonoma County.

Benjamin Taylor, 163. *Photograph*: Petrified Forest, Petrified Forest Rd., c. 6 mi. east of Mark West Springs, Sonoma County.

111 Robert Louis Stevenson, *From Scotland to Silverado* (Cambridge: Belknap, 1966), 198. *Photograph*: Old Faithful Geyser of California, Tubbs Lane, Calistoga, Napa County.

Stevenson, 198. *Photograph*: Brannan cottage, 109 Wapoo Ave., Calistoga, Napa County.

112 Stevenson, 197. *Photograph*: Red Hill, c. 7 mi. northeast on Pine Flat Rd. from Hwy. 128 near Jimtown, Sonoma County.

113 *Santa Cruz Surf* (weekly), October 22, 1892, 6. *Photographs*: Felton Covered Bridge, Felton, c. 6 mi. north on Hwy. 9 from Santa Cruz, Santa Cruz County.

On the Threshold

114 Chapter opening quotation from Theodore Roosevelt, *California Addresses* (San Francisco: California Promotion Committee, 1903), 140. *Illustration*: by Maynard Dixon from *Undaunted* (San Francisco: 1915), a souvenir booklet of poems commemorating the Panama-Pacific International Exposition. *Photograph*: plates fused in the fire of 1906, San Francisco Archives.

116 Albert Gray, "The Plain of Oaks," in *West of the Rocky Mountains*, 410.

117 Hubert Howe Bancroft, *History of the Life of Leland Stanford* (Oakland: Biobooks, 1952), 136.

118 John Galen Howard, as quoted in the *San Francisco Examiner*, November 19, 1902, 9.

119 P. Barrett, an editor of the *San Francisco Examiner*, as quoted in Robert Kirsch and William S. Murphy, *West of the West* (New York, Dutton, 1967), 496. Reprinted by permission of the *San Francisco Examiner*. *Photograph*: Flood Building, Market and Powell streets, San Francisco.

San Francisco Bulletin, April 21, 1906, 1. *Photograph*: Donahue Monument (1906 photograph), sculpted in 1894 by Douglas Tilden, Market and Battery streets, San Francisco. Courtesy San Francisco Archives.

120 Elizabeth Haight Strong, "San Francisco's Upbuilding," *Sunset*, December 1906, 117. Reprinted with permission of Lane Publishing, Menlo Park. *Photograph*: Chinatown, Grant Ave., San Francisco.

121 Louis Christian Mullgardt, as quoted in *The Architecture and Landscape Gardening of the Exposition* (San Francisco: Elder, 1915), v.

122 *Photograph*: Keeler studio, 1736 Highland Place, Berkeley, Alameda County.

123 Charles Keeler, *The Simple Home* (San Francisco: Elder, 1904), 36.

Phil Katz, as quoted in the *San Francisco Chronicle*, © San Francisco Chronicle, October 1, 1924, 7. Reprinted by permission.

John Muir, *The Yosemite* (New York: Doubleday, 1962), 202. *Photograph*: Pulgas Water Temple, Canada Rd., c. 3 mi. south from Hwy. 92, San Mateo County.

124 Charles Keeler, *San Francisco and Thereabout* (San Francisco: Robertson, 1906), 80. *Photograph*: erosion, public open space behind waste treatment plant on Canal Rd., Richmond, Contra Costa County.

Benjamin Ide Wheeler, as quoted in William Bronson, *How to Kill a Golden State* (New York: Doubleday, 1968), 221. Reprinted by permission. *Photograph:* rock crusher (fell in a storm, 1983), north of Richmond–San Rafael Bridge toll plaza, Contra Costa County.

125 Delphin M. Delmas, as quoted in Lawrence Kinnaird, *History of the Greater San Francisco Bay Region* (New York: Lewis Historical Publishing, 1966), vol. 2, 364.

126 Cedric Wright, "High Trip Gleanings," *Sierra Club Bulletin* (San Francisco) 20:1 (February 1935), 32–35. Reprinted by permission. Quotation rearranged in verse form. *Photograph:* Spirit Rock, north side of Sir Francis Drake Hwy., east end of San Geronimo Valley, Marin County. On private property.

127 Luther Burbank, as quoted in Ken Kraft, *Luther Burbank* (New York: Meredith, 1967), 69. *Photograph:* Luther Burbank Gardens, Santa Rosa Recreation and Parks Department, Santa Rosa and Sonoma avenues, Santa Rosa, Sonoma County.

128 *Photograph:* combine-harvester, in possession of Clifford W. Koster, Tracy, San Joaquin County.

129 Edwin Markham, *California the Wonderful* (New York: Hearst's International Library, 1915), 164.

Nellie Denman, as quoted in E. J. Wickson, *Rural California* (New York: MacMillan, 1923), 275.

130 N. B. Scofield, "Shrimp Fisheries of California," *California Fish and Game* 5:1 (January 1919), 6–9. *Photograph:* China Camp State Park, Marin County.

131 Chinese immigrant, as quoted in Him Mark Lai, Genny Lim, and Judy Yung, *Island* (San Francisco: HOC DOI, 1980), 58. Reprinted by permission.

132 Sea shanty, as quoted in display at the National Maritime Museum, San Francisco.

Drawing: rigging plan of *Star of Alaska,* 1909 drawing by C. A. Halvorson, redrawn 1944 by F. W. Shaw, courtesy National Maritime Museum Library.

133 A. J. Petsche, as quoted in the *Oakland Tribune,* March 5, 1933. *Photograph:* Drawbridge ghost town, on Station Island between Coyote Creek and Mud Slough, Alameda County. Accessible only with San Francisco Bay National Wildlife Refuge tours.

134 *San Francisco Examiner,* December 4, 1923, 1.

Sausalito News, 1926, as quoted in Jack Tracy, *Sausalito, Moments in Time* (Sausalito: Windgate, 1983), 146.

135 Joseph Strauss, "The Mighty Task is Done," on a printed card in possession of the San Francisco Archives. Three verses omitted.

In Our Hands

136 David Peri, as quoted in Tracy Salcedo, "Tale of a Lost Race—the Coastal Miwok Indians," *The Fax* (Fairfax), November 14, 1984, 7. *Illustration:* by 9-year-old Trevor Kinsel and 11-year-old Scott Emerick of Marin County.

138 Joseph Fabry, *Swing Shift* (San Francisco: Strawberry Hill, 1982), 199. Reprinted by permission.

139 Malvina Reynolds, from the song "Little Boxes." Words and music by Malvina Reynolds, © 1962 by Schroder Music Co. (ASCAP). Used by permission. All rights reserved. *Photograph:* housing, Serramonte, San Mateo County.

140 Karl Belser, "The Making of Slurban America," *Cry California* (San Francisco) 5:4 (Fall 1970), 17–18. Reprinted by permission. *Photograph:* Santa Clara Valley, view west from

Sierra Rd., Santa Clara County.

Chiang Yee, *The Silent Traveller in San Francisco,* 23. By permission of W. W. Norton and Company, Inc., © 1964 by W. W. Norton and Company, Inc., New York.

141 Editors of Sunset Books and *Sunset* magazine, *Landscaping for Western Living* (Menlo Park: Lane, 1958), 2. Reprinted with permission of the publisher. *Photograph:* Lane Publishing Co. with olive tree planted in 1951, 80 Willow Rd., Menlo Park, San Mateo County. Open to visitors.

142 Joseph H. Engbeck, Jr., *State Parks of California from 1864 to the Present* (Portland: Graphic Arts Center, 1980), 127. Reprinted by permission.

143 Joe Carcione, interview with the author, August 1986. *Photograph:* Voge Ten-Fruit Ranch, 1430 Hollman Lane, Sebastopol, Sonoma County. Open for picking in season.

145 San Franciscans for Reasonable Growth, "So What's Up with Downtown? The Downtown Plan, A Citizen's Critique," prepared for teach-in, as quoted in Chester Hartman, *The Transformation of San Francisco* (Totowa, N.J.: Rowman and Allanheld, 1984), 275. Reprinted by permission of SFRG.

Jack Wickert and Bonnie Sherk, "The Farm: Celery in the Culvert," in *Reinhabiting a Separate Country,* ed. Peter Berg (San Francisco: Planet Drum Foundation, 1978), 138. Reprinted by permission. *Photograph:* Crossroads Community ("The Farm"), 1499 Potrero Ave., San Francisco.

146 Frisco Bay Mussel Group, "Living Here," in Berg, 129. Reprinted by permission.

Yosemite National Institutes, "Ecocenter," brochure in print, 1986. Reprinted by permission. *Photograph:* student and

frog skeleton, Mill Valley Middle School, Marin Co.

147 Robert D. Brown, Jr., and William K. Kockelman, *Geologic Principles for Prudent Land Use,* United States Geological Survey Professional Paper 946, 1983, 2.

148 Tom Stienstra, *San Francisco Examiner,* October 24, 1984, F3. Reprinted by permission.

149 People for Open Space, *Endangered Harvest* (San Francisco: People for Open Space, 1980), 5. Reprinted by permission. *Photograph:* cattle roundup, Diablo Ranch, Mount Diablo, Contra Costa County.

150 Richard Reinhardt, "San Francisco's Shoreline," *Cry California* (San Francisco) 6:2 (Spring 1971), 14. Reprinted by permission. *Photograph:* cliffs, view east from near Land's End to Seacliff, San Francisco.

"San Francisco," *Holiday,* March 1970, 41. Reprinted with permission of *Travel Holiday,* Travel Building, Floral Park, New York 11001.

153 Chiang Yee, *The Silent Traveller in San Francisco,* 281. By permission of W. W. Norton and Company Inc., © 1964 by W. W. Norton and Company Inc., New York. Four lines edited by permission of the publisher.

Robert F. Heizer and Albert B. Elsasser, *The Natural World of the California Indian* (Berkeley and Los Angeles: University of California Press, 1980), 236. Reprinted by permission.

154 Golden Gate National Recreation Area, brochure in print, 1986.

155 Richard Lillard, "The Soil Beneath the Blacktop," in *The California Revolution,* ed. Carey McWilliams (New York: Grossman, 1968), 158. *Photograph:* San Francisco, view from San Bruno Mountain Park, San Mateo County.